THE HUMAN SIDE OF SUCCESS

The author's profit from this book will be donated directly by the publisher to Fundação Solidariedade, one of the social projects maintained by Volvo do Brasil.

Carlos Morassutti

THE HUMAN SIDE OF SUCCESS

How Volvo do Brasil became
a world-class company and one of
the best to work for in the country

Translated from the Portuguese by
José Alvaro de Botelho Néia

EDITORA
ALAÚDE

PROOFREADING:
Rosane Ruth Galle, Ricardo Chut

COVER AND GRAPHIC DESIGN:
Rodrigo Frazão

COVER AND CONTENT PHOTOS:
Silvio Aurichio

PRINTING AND FINISHING:
Bartira Gráfica

1st edition, 2013

Dados Internacionais de Catalogação na Publicação (CIP)
(Câmara Brasileira do Livro, SP , Brasil)

Morassutti, Carlos
The human side of success : how Volvo do Brasil became a world-class company and one of the best to work for in the country / Carlos Morassutti ; [translation José Álvaro de Botelho Néia]. -- São Paulo : Alaúde Editorial, 2012.
Título original: O lado humano do sucesso : como a Volvo do Brasil se tornou uma empresa de classe mundial e uma das melhores do país para trabalhar.

ISBN 978-85-7881-152-5

1. Volvo do Brasil (Empresa) - História I. Título.

12-12489 CDD-338.470981

Índices para catálogo sistemático:
1. Volvo do Brasil : Grupo empresarial : História 338.470981

2013
Alaúde Editorial Ltda.
Rua Hildebrando Thomaz de Carvalho, 60
04012-120, São Paulo, SP, Brasil
Tel.: (+55 11) 5572-9474 e 5579-6757
www.alaude.com.br

I dedicate this book to Giancarlo and Lucca,
my sons, and to Madelon, my wife.
They are the passion that drives my life.

Contents

Foreword

I have lived intensely every moment of this history – not as a mere spectator, but as an active participant. In fact, I helped to build it. I trod on mud to see up close the construction of the factory. Filled with pride, I waved the Brazilian flag when the president of the country at that time, João Baptista Figueiredo, inaugurated it. I watched, with emotion, the first bus come out of the assembly line in 1979 and, in the following year, the first truck.

I was a privileged observer. Given the role I had at the time, I knew every employee by name and ID number. I delivered every pay slip personally to each one. This allowed me to walk every corner of the plant. I was able to watch it take shape and grow at each day.

Since then, more than thirty years have passed, along which thousands of trucks and buses were manufactured and marketed. Volvo do Brasil became a high-performance, world-class company. It earned the respect of different audiences and, today, has become a reference in Brazil and in the Volvo world.

As for me, I also took on new challenges until I became a member of the company board. For over two decades in this post, I participate actively in every decision with impact on the paths of the organization. I had the privilege of working for every president of Volvo do Brasil. I am the only member that survived the different compositions that the board had since I joined it. And, unfortunately, I no longer know every employee personally, nor do I know their ID numbers by heart, because there are now thousands of them.

Time has passed, but it feels like it was yesterday. The memories of all that I lived still dwell in my mind and in my heart, even the most distant ones: my childhood, my first job, and the dream of a successful career in a large company. Many things have happened over the course of the years. And, little by little, life taught me the lessons I needed to learn to accomplish my dreams.

At Volvo, I started building my professional career step by step. I grew and developed together with the company. I dare say that, in some moments, our stories interlaced with each other. For this reason, and also given the huge pride I feel at having experienced all this, I believe I have legitimacy to tell a bit of this story.

I confess that, in the beginning, I thought this idea seemed quite insane. But what other choice did I have? My physician had just told me I would have to stay three or four months without doing any physical activity, because of a small urgent surgery on my leg. Plus I had scheduled family vacations following that. And, of course, I had every intention to put my body in movement. I am not the type to stand still. Not doing physical exercises is just unthinkable for me – mission nearly impossible.

Later, when I realized there was really no way out of it, I decided that only a major challenge, that would keep my mind busy and would not require major physical efforts, could get me out of this trouble. So I thought about taking an intensive course in yoga and meditation, but I felt that was too radical. I'm not ready for that yet. That's when the idea of the book came up.

The more I thought about this possibility, the more enthusiastic I became. Finally, already taken by the adrenaline, I decided to face the challenge. And in the same way as I had faced so many others: with clear objectives, rules, and assumptions.

I established for myself that the book would have to be written during the month I was on vacation. If more time was needed, I would use the one I usually dedicate to physical activities, with a three-month limit to conclude the challenge. I should write as if I were practicing a sport that I enjoy – that is, in a pleasant way.

With a simple and direct language, the book should approach the human side of the organization that, in my opinion, is decisive for its success and focus on the things that worked out right. Based solely on my experiences in the corporate world and personal life, I should be able to answer two basic questions which are often asked me: "How did Volvo do Brasil build its history of success?" and "How did you build such a successful career remaining in the same area and in the same company for so long?" To do this, I should retrieve the memory of the most striking moments in Volvo do Brasil's trajectory and the learning that I had over the course of my life.

Finally, I should convince Rosane, my assistant and "trusted aide", to embark with me on this challenge. After so many years working together, she has developed the blessed capability of capturing exactly what I want to say – or would like to have said. With her serenity offsetting my anxiety, she would be the right person to help me put on paper, in a clear and accurate form, the ideas that were already beginning to bubble up in my mind and stir my heart.

As you can see, the targets were very ambitious. In fact, they were too ambitious. Like the typical truck driver on the first trip, I thought that writing a book would be easy and quick and that I could do it with my hand behind my back. All I needed was to have the whole story in my mind and apply my usual determination in overcoming challenges. But in practice it wasn't like this.

Soon I realized that just using the time I dedicated to physical activities wouldn't be enough. So, in parallel to the busy day-to-day life at the company, I started writing in the evenings, weekends, and holidays. Even so, it took double the time that I had initially stipulated to conclude this challenge. That is, it took six months for the book to be ready – which is still a very reasonable timeframe for such a complex task requiring so much reflection. On the other hand, I had the pleasure of retaking physical activities before the deadline set by the doctor – for pure stubbornness.

After such a rush, the result of all this work is here, in your hands, and brings with it the sweet taste of victory. The wonderful feeling of "mission accomplished". I hope that, in some way, it will be able to add value to all those who live in the complex – and passionate – corporate world. I also hope that it may serve as an inspiration to all those who carry in their blood the spirit of the warrior, the ongoing quest for excellence, and the calling to accomplish.

The challenge of reading this book is now in your hands. Will you take it? If you do, I hope that at the end you will feel that it was worthwhile – the same feeling I had when I finished writing it.

Carlos Morassutti

Acknowledgements

Building Volvo do Brazil was a dream - in the beginning, of a few. But it gradually infected other people and awoke in them a huge desire to be part of a story that was beginning to be written. Some were in the front line, others acted indirectly, but everyone contributed.

After accomplishing the initial dream, many others came along, and more people arrived adding their efforts to transforming these into reality. Today, they number in the thousands. I would like to be able to mention their names individually - in particular of those who contributed in a more substantial way. If it were not for them, there would be no story to tell. Since this would be a practically impossible task, I would like to leave my gratitude collectively:

To all those who believed that Volvo do Brasil was a possible dream, beginning by the creators of the project in Sweden and by the pioneers who arrived here to make it happen.

To all the presidents of Volvo do Brasil who, imbued of the Viking warriors' spirit, led the company during storms and doldrums all the way until today. Each one, in his own way, left his mark and contributed for us to become what we are today. With all of them I learned, and the lessons were different - some were extremely marking.

To the employees, of all times, who dedicated their work and energy to the company. To those who spent here an entire life and to those who were here just for a season. To all those who are part of the current moment and who, with a lot of passion, competence, and commitment, bring our plans and dreams to life.

To all outsourced workers, consultants, suppliers, dealers, importers, and other partners of our business chain who have complemented us along the years with their competencies and commitment. And to those who, nowadays, form with us a winning team.

To all the customers who trust in our brand and carry on buying our products.

To all the audiences who have with us a relationship based on professionalism, respect, and ethics.

To all the people who follow the trajectory of Volvo do Brasil and root for our success.

To my parents, for having taught me the value of work, humbleness, and persistence.

To all those I met in my life and who, in some way, helped me to take that additional step, to go beyond, to evolve as a person and as a professional.

To all my friends who kindly read this book with the task of telling me honestly whether it should be published or simply put away in a drawer. Their comments and suggestions were really valuable to me.

And, finally, to my family for the understanding and support throughout the period in which I dove head-first into the inebriating task of writing and overcoming one more challenge.

A very special thank you

In a special way, I would like to thank Rosane Ruth Galle for the partnership and the companionship during all these years of corporate life. And, above all, for having dived with me into the challenging, exhaustive, and extremely moving experience of writing a book for the first time.

With competence, sensitivity, and a lot of patience, Rosane polished the texts I gave her. She removed the excesses and clarified the obscure parts, giving them shine and color. At the same time, she contributed with suggestions and perceptions, outcomes of her professional experience and of her journey on the trail of self-knowledge. She would certainly be able to spend a month meditating and doing yoga. This challenge I still owe her.

Anyway, I would like to make a record here of my "thank you very much" for the unique work she has performed - typical of the dedicated professionals who know how to make the difference and who leave their mark on everything they do.

Introduction

The more I live in the corporate world, the more I see lessons on how to be successful in the organizational and personal spheres to be given. Several formulas are announced. Even though the clothing might be new, they all end up basically saying the same things, because the essence is the same. And there is nothing wrong with that. In truth, it is the essence that counts and makes the difference.

Success is pursued by everyone and in every way. The customer and the product quality always appear as the main focus, the main reason for the existence of companies. They all depend on these factors to be successful. That is why actions are always targeted at satisfying and charming customers. On the personal side, the fact that people should take on the responsibility for their success is always emphasized.

At Volvo do Brasil it is no different. Exceeding the expectations of our customers and anticipating their demands for tomorrow are permanent items on our agenda. We also encourage employees to take on the responsibility for their careers and for the other dimensions of their lives. We make it clear that this should never be delegated to the company or to anyone else.

Like the majority of organizations, we have a solid organizational structure and all the necessary resources and tools for sustainable business management. In addition, we have strategic plans for production, products, marketing, investment and so on. There are plans and more plans in every area. Most of them work - a few, not quite.

We basically face the same difficulties found in any business environment. We commit mistakes and mismatches. We are not perfect, nor do we want to be seen as such.

In summary, we are very similar to any other organization in most aspects. And these are not the points that I approach in this book. Instead, I report on what differentiates us as a company and that is part of our essence, without having the pretension of giving any sort of magic success formula. We do not have one anyway.

I deliberately focused on the positive points that leveraged the development of Volvo do Brasil, placing it at the level of world-class organizations and at the top of the ranking of the best companies to work for in Brazil for several years in a row. Why? Simply for believing that it is the strengths that support organizations and people, making them grow.

This book is split into five parts. The first one, **The Taste of Victory**, describes in a very brief way the company's trajectory to success. In quick brushstrokes, I show the main accomplishments we have had over the years.

But how did we get there? The answer is in the second part – **The Secrets of Success**. To my way of seeing, ten factors took us to the level of a world-class, high-performance company. Each one has its own value in isolation. However, it was all of them together that made the difference in our journey.

In the third part, **World-Class People**, I reveal the biggest secret to our success, the one which enables us to have highly motivated and engaged employees - the master key that opens any door to the success of an organization.

In **World-Class Environment**, Part IV, I explain which were the tools and resources that we deployed to establish the factors that led us to success and what we do to maintain them.

Finally, I risk making a few projections, even without a crystal ball. In the last part, **A Look to the Future**, I mention some of the challenges and opportunities that we have ahead of us in our segment of activity, based on the trends of the current world.

From a business perspective, these are the main points I approach in this book. But there is much more. Over the course of the narrative, I draw several parallels between my career and personal life, sharing the lessons that I learned as time went by.

Perhaps this learning can serve as reference for people who are looking for the stepping stones to the corporate world or for those who are striving for development and self-fulfillment in any other context. But there is no way to know that for sure. Each one has to evaluate and come to their own conclusions.

Having said that, I can only wish you a good reading!

Prêmio Nacional
da Qualidade

PART I

THE TASTE OF VICTORY

1

Pride of the Large Group

They came in a relaxed manner, dragging their clogs of different colors and models as if they were at home. They drew the attention of the less informed people, in particular when they wore their clogs with suits. A weird combination for our standards, but perfectly aligned with the fashion in their culture in the late 1970s.

They dared to be different – not only in what they wore but also in their behavior. They held the cutlery in a peculiar way. They chewed tobacco without ceremony. They wore the safety belts in cars in a country where no one even thought about that. They respected the traffic laws and any other current legislation. They treated people with respect. They were not at all reminiscent of the fearsome Viking warriors of the stories that we had heard.

The local community identified them as "the Swedes from Volvo". What no one was exactly sure of was what Volvo did or the plans it had. This awoke people's curiosity and imagination. But, in reality, the mission of the Swedes was very clear and accurately defined: to build a truck and bus manufacturer called Volvo do Brasil.

The strangeness caused by the first contacts we had with them quickly became admiration and, after that, pride, as we were told the history of the Volvo Group and its culture was passed on.

Pride is, without any doubt, the word that best describes the feeling we had since the very beginning for belonging to a global organization with an impressive successful history.

And this history began with the dream of two visionary Swedes of producing an automobile capable of traveling safely on the roads of Sweden. The weather conditions there were very harsh and there was snow for a good part of the year. In the summer of 1924, in a restaurant in Stockholm, they began discussing the guidelines for the establishment of the company.

In less than three years, the first car came out of the assembly line. It was christened Jacob. The small company, located in Gothenburg, received the name of Volvo, which in Latin means "I roll". The logo was the symbol of iron, which was utilized to make the Swedish steel used in manufacturing the vehicles and recognized for its strength and quality.

Assar Gabrielsson, an economist, and Gustaf Larsson, an engineer, needed a lot of courage and determination to transform their dream into reality. They were true entrepreneurs at a time in which the world did not even know this expression.

The small company grew and developed over the years until it became the Volvo Group, which diversified its activities and began to operate in different segments. Today, adjusted to the new times, it is focused on the commercial automotive and heavy construction segments. Its main objective is to provide sustainable transport solutions. In spite of having begun its history as a manufacturer of automobiles, the Group is currently one of the world's largest truck manufacturers. It comprises the brands Volvo, Mack, Renault, UD, and Eicher.

In addition to trucks, currently representing approximately 70 percent of the business, Volvo manufactures buses, construction equipment, and marine engines that, added to financial services, generate revenues higher than the GDP of many countries.

The Group is present in every continent and in over a hundred and eighty countries. It has plants in many of them and approximately 100,000 employees spread out around the world. It represents a strong brand, well respected in its segment of activity, which has become a reference in safety and quality.

Since it was established, Volvo has always emphasized that vehicles are produced by people and for transporting people. Therefore, safety is fundamental – both for those who manufacture the vehicles and for those who will drive them. It was the Group that invented the three-point safety belt and launched the airbag for trucks in Brazil. In addition to safety, quality and respect for the environment are also core values of the Group. When the issue is emissions, the company states openly, "We are part of the problem, but also of the solution."

At Volvo do Brasil, the Group's values and special way of behaving in the business world, which have always placed it in the lead, filled us with pride. And they were clearly felt in the way we were treated: with a lot of consideration and respect. We were enchanted. We constantly repeated how wonderful it was to work for and be part of this great group.

For a long time, we saw expatriates arriving and leaving. The Swedes were the vast majority. They left here many teachings. In their baggage on the return, they took more than pleasant memories of a happy country, with samba, football, and *caipirinha*. They also took the certainty that the company had a promising future. Most of them were really missed after they left.

Our admiration for the Volvo Group also extended to its country of origin. By Brazilian standards, Sweden is a small country. It is practically the size of the state of Paraná, where we are located, and has approximately the same population. But it is very powerful. It has big companies in different segments and operations throughout the world.

Open to diversity, the Swedes have always employed women in their factories. They see the fact that both in the couple work out and share the responsibility for raising the children and for the domestic chores as only natural.

In addition to respect for people, the Swedish culture is characterized by care for the environment. The Swedes love to sail and to be close to nature. They take advantage of any and every opportunity to sunbathe, because the king star appears very little on their sky. In winter, it usually gets dark at around three o'clock in the afternoon. In summer, the temperature hardly exceeds 25 degrees Celsius. This explains the fact that the Swedes, back then in Brazil, used to relax on the lawn in front of our plant, during lunchtime, whenever the sun was out – to the surprise of the Brazilians, more formal and used to having the sun all year round.

The Swedes are concerned with society and sustainability. They respect each other's space. They look for consensus in every decision, even if this takes a little longer. They trust in people. They act with responsibility both in the corporate world and in society.

The Swedish culture reflected in the Volvo Group, with consistent management practices, business ethics, and long-term sustainable vision, only fueled our admiration. In addition to the passion for football, which the Swedes had in common with us, there was only the fact that Queen Silvia spoke our language – for having had a Brazilian mother and lived in Brazil.

The dream of the Brazilians involved in the initial project for building Volvo do Brasil was to be able to visit Sweden one day. Everyone wanted to see from up close what we were always being told. Whenever this happened, it was a reason for celebration on the departure and on the return of the employee – with entitlement to a feature article in the company in-house newsletter, richly illustrated with the pictures from a distant and fascinating world.

With me, it was no different. The opportunity to visit Sweden came through a three-month program, whose objective was to visit the plants and see from up close what the Human Resources practices were. I discovered a totally new world that I had never imagined – and not just in Human Resources. I saw high technology in the plants, with robots and electric dollies that had sensors and stopped whenever there was anyone in front; workers in the plants of Udevala and Kalmar, including women, who assembled complete automobiles and not just isolated parts as it happens in serial production; self-managed teams that determined their own shifts, workdays, and form of production; flexible working hours, controlled by the employees with the aid of a special ruler; labor union representatives with a business view and a place in the board – all of this in the early 1980s.

It was clear to me that the Swedes had thought of everything, because everything worked. Beginning by the respect in traffic: whenever I wanted to cross a street, cars stopped like the electric dollies in the plants. There were novelties everywhere: in the infrastructure, in the products, in the supermarket, and in stores in general.

In the companies, there was no big difference between the salary of the bosses and those of their subordinates. For this reason, many people did not have the ambition of taking on leadership roles. In addition to that, with the salary raise, they would be forced to pay a higher tax percentage, which ended up not being attractive in financial terms. The taxes levied from the employees were really high, but well deployed by the government in infrastructure, health, education, and other benefits.

However, what really drew my attention were the people and the respect that they had for others. I was extremely well treated and was received by everyone exactly as it was in the program. And punctually! Punctuality is another strong point of the Swedish culture.

Since my English was not that good, I used to read Sidney Sheldon to practice and enrich my vocabulary. In addition to helping me with the language, the books reinforced my belief that nothing in life is free. The heroines went through terrible moments. They sweated, worked hard, but always managed to get through. They were a tremendous inspiration!

Not even the bad climate bothered me. The falling snow enchanted me. I had never seen this before. The feeling was nearly the same as when I saw the sea and stepped on the sand of the beach for the first time, already an adult then. And now, for the first time outside Brazil, everything was a discovery, a positive surprise, and huge learning.

I saw what I had come to see in the area of Human Resources and visited the plants I was supposed to visit. In one of them, they even flew the Brazilian flag. I thought with myself: "Gosh, who would've said that a hick like me – who a little while ago left home with a backpack, no definite destination, and nothing to my name – would travel so far and would receive so many honors!" The image of the Brazilian flag flying in such a distant country to receive Brazilians caused in me an unforgettable feeling.

When I returned to Brazil, I realized that I was fully engaged and infected by the Volvo spirit. I had experienced a new world and this only increased my admiration and respect for the Group and for Sweden. I was ready to fly the flag of both countries, together with Volvo's, and bravely face all the challenges that might come our way.

This was also the prevailing feeling in the majority of the company's employees. The pride only increased over time and with the interaction with the Swedes. Like the son who wants to be like his successful father, with sound moral and ethical values, we also mirrored ourselves in the Volvo Group and in Sweden and dreamed of one day establishing a successful company in a better Brazil. This made our hearts beat stronger and to the rhythm of the Viking warriors – the invincible conquerors and courageous explorers. We were so thrilled that many Brazilians began wearing clogs.

2

Mutual pride

Given that the world is always spinning and life is going its own roundabout way, sometimes the improbable thing happens. And it did: in recent years, it was the Volvo Group that became immensely proud of Volvo do Brasil. Not just for the results we have achieved and what this came to represent for the Group, but in particular because we have become a reference of excellence in the Volvo world – thanks to the set of practices adopted here, to the high level of professionalism, and to all the accomplishments of recent years. This means that the pride we have always had of the Volvo Group began to be mutual. It became truly reciprocal.

We still receive many Swedes and other foreigners at Volvo do Brasil, but now they don't come only to teach. They also come to learn. They want to see and understand what we are doing. They leave amazed. Without any embarrassment, they say out loud that we are an example to be followed. They make speeches praising our achievements and results, which of course flatters us. They bring customers, leaders from the top management, and different audiences to see from up close our practices and the plant that produces vehicles with one of the Group's highest quality rates.

Formerly, foreigners also learned with us, but they learned what not to do. The country was living under sky-high inflation, going through different government plans, constant changes of currency, price controls, conversion tables, many uncertainties, and all that a crazy and out-of-control economy can generate – not to mention the high level of corruption and the business practices out of compliance with the Volvo standards. All this constantly jeopardized the continuity of the business in the country. Brazil was a backward school: here they learned what they should not do. Attending this school was practically mandatory for foreigners who wanted to make a career in the Group, mainly in the financial area.

Today, however, we have the true "Brazilian school". We teach good practices and procedures, not only to the foreigners who come here but also to any professional wishing to learn in a world-class business environment. Many people that hold, or have held, the highest positions in the Volvo Group have already passed by here.

Previously, the respect and admiration of the Swedes from the Volvo Group for Brazilians was limited to football. Sweden had been the venue for the 1958 FIFA World Cup and, on that occasion, Pelé and the Brazilian national team charmed everyone. The entire audience applauded them standing up, even seeing Sweden lose the game and the world title to Brazil.

The Swedes who lived here also began to admire the creativity, the commitment, and mainly the Brazilians' happy and relaxed way of being. A good barbecue and a few *caipirinhas* were enough for everyone to have fun. And right there, plans were made to the beach, to a football match, and even to Carnival.

Today, the pride they feel is for a world-class organization that they helped to shape and develop. This is similar to a father who was able to encourage, pass on values, charge responsibilities, and later on recognizes happily that his son is able to walk on his own legs and be as good as he is – or even surpass him. After all, the apple doesn't fall far from the tree.

My parents felt a similar pride when I brought them from the countryside for a better life in the big city. They realized I had made it and was capable of walking on my own legs. My father had been very tough with me when I decided to leave home. He said in an exalted tone that I would go hungry and come back in a hurry.

In a way, he was right: I did go hungry. But I didn't go back. His words served as challenge and motivation and, added to the values that he had passed down to me, drove me towards my objectives. And, deep inside, I knew that his harsh words had been motivated by his protective instinct. He feared for what could happen to me. After all, I was going out into the world and knew nothing about it. Even though he wasn't able to verbalize this, nor did he say goodbye to me, I clearly felt his love when I saw him hiding behind a column at the bus station as the bus departed. That was his silent way of bidding me farewell and wishing me good luck.

For Volvo do Brasil, it is also very important to feel that the head office is proud of it, of the way it acts, and of the results it delivers. This is the dream of any subsidiary. And it only became a reality because we were able to count on many people who worked hard, believed, placed their hopes, and rooted for the company to work out right. As usual, there were also some people who were against it and, in some moments, defended the idea that this unit should be closed down and that the Volvo Group should leave the country. But this only gave us more strength and courage to continue on our journey.

The young Swede who disembarked here in the early 1970s, to check out the feasibility of building a plant in Brazil, certainly never imagined that we would go so far. Traveling in a Volkswagen Beetle all over the country, he counted trucks by the roadside. His objective was to map all the business opportunities to later present them in Sweden, so that the head office could decide whether to take the project forward or not. In this same period, the possibility of manufacturing buses for the city of Curitiba arose, as an innovative project in the area of public transportation was just starting. As a result of all that, the young man not only received the green light for the project but also became the first president of Volvo do Brasil.

Decision made, the location of the plant had to be defined. With the federal government's intention of decentralizing the automotive industry, basically concentrated on the Rio – São Paulo axis, countless possibilities were raised. Campinas, Porto Alegre, and Curitiba were the cities with the best chances.

Curitiba ended up being the chosen city. The closeness to the Port of Paranaguá, the incipient industrial district, the technical schools that provided a good level of manpower, the population that in its majority was descended from immigrants and had a way of living somewhat similar to that of European countries were decisive factors in this decision. What really weighed, though, was the interest and support from the authorities at the time. The city and state secretaries, the mayor, the governor, and even the Minister of Treasury were tireless defenders of the idea of building the Volvo plant in Curitiba.

With everyone's blessing, Volvo do Brasil was finally established on October 24, 1977. In that same year, the operations of Volvo Penta, the marine and industrial engine division, started in Rio de Janeiro. Volvo Construction Equipment in Pederneiras, state of São Paulo, came a bit later. In 1987, due to the merger of Volvo to Clark Michigan and Euclid, Volvo Michigan Euclid (VME) was established. In 1995, Volvo took over the entire business and the company received the name of Volvo Construction Equipment.

The Volvo trucks, however, were already well known in Brazil for a long time. They had been exported here for nearly three decades: from the early 1930s to the beginning of the 1960s, when the Brazilian government limited importations and began to stimulate the development of a national automotive park.

Even throughout the Second World War, the trucks kept on coming. And this required a lot of juggling: some trucks went to Asia first, then to the United States, and finally disembarked in Brazil. Manufactured in real Swedish steel, the best at that time, they were known for being robust and resistant. The excellent quality and the high level of technology also drew people's attention.

In the early 1950s, a truck and bus manufacturing unit was almost established in Brazilian territory. Assar Gabrielsson, in his second visit to Brazil, left the country convinced that this would be a great place for this type of venture. The project progressed and the venue defined was São José dos Campos, in the state of São Paulo. However, the political and economic instability caused by the tragic death of the president of Brazil, Getúlio Vargas, made him put the project on hold.

But the dream persisted and ended up materializing more than twenty years later, when Volvo do Brasil was finally established in Curitiba and appropriately set up in the "White House" – as the house on Mateus Leme Street was known. That is where the central office was set up and where I went to work.

The beginning was extremely challenging and filled with obstacles, but also loaded with opportunities. Everything had to be done: hire personnel, create policies and procedures aligned with the Volvo Group, build the plant, and develop the supply chain and the dealer network. In short, work and more hard work.

Life moved on, the world went round, the Volvo Group underwent changes, and both Brazilian and Swedish societies changed. In the middle of all this, Volvo do Brasil built its history and showed that the decision of establishing the plant in Curitiba was right, given that several other companies ended up coming here after that. In the last decade, an important automotive hub consolidated in the region.

Today, Volvo do Brasil is responsible for the business of the Volvo Group in all Latin America and has more than 6,000 employees spread throughout this territory. We manufacture thousands of trucks, buses, and construction equipment every year, with significant revenues and results for the Group. Our business chain runs at full steam, with qualified suppliers, a competent dealer network, engaged employees, and satisfied customers.

At the manufacturing complex in Curitiba, we assemble trucks and bus chassis. In addition to supplying the Brazilian market, they are exported to all Latin America and to other countries around the world. This is not bad for a company that, for many years, was mentioned in the head office reports and presentations in the class known as RoW (*rest of the world*) – comprised by the countries in the Group that did not post sufficient results to have their figures reported separately – fearing that at any moment the operation could be closed for "rounding", as some people used to joke about.

There were many changes over all these years. However, our admiration and respect for the Volvo Group and for its leaders remained unchanged. Perhaps just the initial enchantment for the novelty of an entirely new world has dissipated. Now we are also part of this world and have access to things that before we did not – including the imported products that so drew my attention on my first trip to Sweden. By the way, traveling to Sweden and other countries has become something ordinary, even for recently hired employees. It ceased to be a reason for a celebration or for an article in the company newsletter. And it no longer has the same glamour.

We have evolved and gained self-confidence. As a company, we have managed to go far. We have achieved our objectives, accomplished our dreams, and earned recognition. As a country, we have also progressed. We know that the journey ahead is still a long one, but our conditions are not so different anymore from those of Sweden and other developed nations.

When I look around, I clearly perceive how much our employees have grown – and not just in numbers. The level of professional and personal development that they have achieved is also impressive. In general, we have all evolved in our way of thinking and acting. From the initial strangeness towards the Swedes, who seemed to have come from another world, we moved to the perception that they were people just like us, with all the qualities and defects of any human being.

I had the privilege of interacting with practically all the Swedes who passed by here. From those who performed the simplest of functions all the way to the highest levels of senior management. I have talked with presidents of the Volvo Group, with presidents of the shareholders council, and even with Queen Silvia and other Swedish authorities. I have learned that, regardless of their hierarchical position, people are essentially the same all over the world. The only things that change are cultures and customs.

Initially, some Brazilians used to say that the Swedes would rather hug trees than people, as a reference to the cold way in which they greeted us. However, the Swedes I have met along my journey have always shown a high level of sensitivity and a huge heart. They just had a less physical way of demonstrating this in the first moments. After a period working with us, however, many began to greet everyone in a warmer way, like the Brazilians do. For me, the relationship with the Swedes has always been based on deep respect and a high level of consideration, resulting in huge learning.

Today we know that, in addition to the support of the Volvo Group which we have always had, we can also count on their pride for the Brazilian factory and for the way in which we manage our business. They have realized we have reached maturity with our own personality and identity. We are more confident than ever. We have a lot of experience, willingness, and "muscles" to face challenges. And we are ready to take off for even higher flights!

3

The major achievements

We are currently experiencing a very special moment, marked by great results and recognition that will forever remain in Volvo do Brasil's history. It is a moment of glories. We celebrate victories, both collective and individual, in practically all areas of the company.

We are harvesting what we planted. The seeds were sown in a fertile environment of dedication and commitment, which counts on the power of an integrated whole. We know that no accomplishment in the corporate world is the outcome of a single isolated action. Even the individual ones are the outcome of the group work. They are the sum of actions by different areas and people. We value the effort and dedication of all employees. We understand that the contributions are given in different levels, but are complementary to each other. And this is what makes the company stronger.

We also know that the wave of success on which we are surfing right now is owed to the efforts of a sound journey of many years. Brazil is also experiencing an extremely positive phase, which benefits us directly.

We are very proud of our accomplishments. Some were planned in detail. Others were just a consequence of work well done. At any rate, they must all be seen linked together, considering the impact on the whole of the organization, both in the present and in the future. In isolation, they may become just one more victory, with no major effect.

The accomplishments began to appear gradually, one leveraging on the other. We cannot really say what happened first. Our trucks became the object of desire of our customers. This led us to the leadership in the extremely competitive heavy truck segment in Brazil a few times. We were also awarded the title of "most admired company" of the automotive sector several times.

In the last three years, we occupied the position of largest Volvo truck market in the world twice, ahead of other units in the Volvo Group in the United States and in countries of Europe. We know that the world out there has not done too well lately. Nonetheless, we managed to increase significantly the volumes in Brazil and throughout South America. This happened as the result of a very wise decision: to enter the medium-heavy truck segment in 2003. In spite of many people being against it, Volvo do Brasil imposed its will and today we celebrate the results.

This victory was the outcome of the fantastic work done by the staff in the plant and by the entire business chain – in particular the dealers. They are the ones who are in the front line every day, servicing our customers with a high level of dedication and competence. The relationship between Volvo and its dealers, which is based on respect and professionalism, has been recognized by surveys and by the dealers themselves as one of the best among the manufacturers in Brazil.

Consequently, the brand image and the level of satisfaction of our customers are the best in the sector, according to different sources. We work hard to provide the best transport solution that will address not only the needs of our customers but also the desires of their customers.

Consistent practices and respect for people have led us to the "Best Company to Work for" award in Brazil. In the last four years, we have been among the three best companies. In 2008 and 2011, we were the best. We have been given several other prizes and recognitions in this sense, at state and national levels, by institutions of renown. This attests to the high levels of satisfaction and engagement that always appear in the organizational climate surveys carried out by the Volvo Group.

We have one of the Volvo Group's highest levels of quality in vehicle assembly, according to strict and detailed audits carried out continuously by auditors from Sweden. Our current level of quality is acknowledged worldwide.

We have been given the coveted National Brazilian Quality Award (PNQ), which placed us in the world-class company level. We are the only manufacturer in Brazil – in the automobile, bus, and truck category – to have received this award so far.

We took the concept of lean production so seriously and professionally that the results achieved exceeded the expectations. We created the Volvo Industrial System, which was later transformed into a global tool and implemented in the other units of the Group. The responsibility for this global implementation fell to a Brazilian.

By the way, the fact of having so many Brazilians working today in other companies of the Group, many in standout positions, was also a major accomplishment. Our competence began to be recognized all over the world and we ended up becoming a great supplier of expatriates.

In the engine plant, we have achieved high rates in World-Class Manufacturing (WCM) audits. Because of that, we have become a reference and benchmark for the Volvo Group.

Thanks to our performance, we have managed to obtain investments from the Volvo Group to increase and improve our entire manufacturing complex. This has increased our installed capacity significantly. As a consequence, it was possible to establish a gearbox manufacturing unit in 2011 – the only one in the Volvo Group outside Sweden.

Thanks to the competence acquired over the years, we began providing financial, engineering, informatics, and other types of services to the Volvo world. Likewise, some global processes in different areas also started to be managed from Brazil.

The Volvo Construction Equipment plant in Pederneiras has also achieved excellent results and set countless records within the Group. The commercial area, located in Curitiba, has been gaining an increasing share of the Latin American market and, consequently, has enlarged its participation in the Volvo Group.

Volvo Penta, which markets marine and industrial engines, is also consolidating its position as a strong brand in the Brazilian market. Some time ago, its operation base was transferred from Rio de Janeiro to Curitiba.

Volvo Financial Services has stood out on the financial market. With efficiency and a high level of agility, it has been providing support to the Volvo brand's growth throughout Latin America.

We hold the record for the world's longest bus and with the greatest transportation capacity – the bi-articulated bus. It was designed here, with Brazilian technology. The innovation and safety of our vehicles have already yielded us a number of awards. Our buses are part of everyday life in cities and highways. They transport people in comfort and with efficiency.

We have received a number of recognitions, including international ones, for the Volvo Traffic Safety Program. This program, established over twenty years ago, has already mobilized thousands of people for a more humane traffic in Brazil and other countries of South America.

Our workplace diversity programs, our sustainable actions, and our social, cultural, and sports projects have also been the object of local and international recognition. The different awards received, among which the one for "corporate citizen", show us that we are on the right path in this area.

Different trophies adorn the shelves in various departments. They tell a long history of great accomplishments that we have achieved as a company or as an area, in corporate or specific projects. They are the true depiction of our organization's sound and consistent journey in the quest for excellence and serve as inspiration for us to continue forward in large strides. In addition, they are reflected directly in our results. This is extremely important, given that the company does not survive on awards alone.

We have celebrated all these accomplishments together with our employees. Our gratitude ranges from a simple and warm "thank you" for work well done all the way to special luncheons and large festive celebrations with famous artists.

At the same time, we hope that our employees also have many personal accomplishments to celebrate, based on each one's life objectives. We expect them to fight for what they desire and to go in search of their dreams. We strongly believe that a winning company is made up of winning people.

I continually challenge myself to strive for development in other dimensions of my life, in addition to the professional sphere. In order to achieve my targets, I deploy the same tools, concepts, and mental models of the corporate world. And I have enjoyed the same taste of victory.

Professionally, I have reached where I wanted to. I feel happy and completely fulfilled – in particular, given my starting point: an environment of few prospects and a lot of poverty. My father could not read nor write. He believed that his children also had no need to learn. The important thing was working. Thank goodness my mother, even though she did not go to school either, thought differently and was persistent.

As a child, I worked as a shoeshine boy. Then I started to deliver milk and at the age of 13 I joined a company, full-time, as an office-boy – through a local institution program for needy children called Guarda-Mirim (Junior Guard). By the age of 14, I was already a hired employee.

Since then, I have spent more than forty years, practically uninterrupted, in the area of Human Resources. Of these, I have spent over thirty years at Volvo do Brasil. And I can affirm that I am still passionate for this area. My work has been recognized and valued in many different ways, which makes me very happy.

Over two decades ago, I became a member of the board of Volvo do Brasil. I am responsible for the HR & Corporate Affairs division, which includes a number of other corporate areas that I took on as the years passed: Administrative Support; Corporate Communication and Public Relations; Institutional and Government Affairs; Health, Safety, and Environment; Management Systems and Corporate Security; Viking Association; and Vikingprev – the employees' pension fund. For over ten years, I was also responsible for the legal department.

Managing areas so different from each other has been a great challenge, which allows me to discuss a wide range of topics and to get in contact with extremely varied audiences: from the simplest people to the highest authority in the country. Through this, I have developed new competencies and enhanced the ones I already had.

Accomplishments are wonderful both in the personal and in the professional areas, but not everyone can see the effort made to get there. In people's mind there is only the memory of the prize received or the picture of the moment in which the finishing line was crossed. Many times people ask me if it is difficult to run a marathon. I always answer that it is very easy. The difficult thing is to get ready to do it. A lot of practicing is needed – and some sacrifices too.

I managed to obtain everything that a good, simple person dreams of having: respect, a dignified and balanced life, a successful career, and a wonderful family. Today I have a financial condition that allows me to buy the things that I dreamt of having in the past. But now I realize that I no longer need them. There are other things that I have started to value much more: being with my family, spending good moments with friends, managing to improve my performance in a marathon, having the breath and drive to participate in the centennial Paris-Brest-Paris cycling event, having accumulated enough experience to write a book about. My personal objectives and interests have naturally changed over the course of my life. And the old maxim that it is more important to be than to have became totally true.

For me, the definition of success is summarized in the text of a small picture, already faded by the passage of time, that I have on my table in the office: "You can use most any measure when speaking of success. Some measure by the size of their house or the net worth of their portfolio. However, the measure of real success is one you cannot spend... It's the way your child describes you when talking to a friend."

At Volvo, we say all the time that the achievements accomplished must be enjoyed and celebrated, but with the awareness that they are no guarantee of success for challenges that will come up in the future. Other than the aggregate experience, they merely serve as a reference.

The conditions and the world are constantly changing. And to continue being successful, it may be necessary to paddle all over again in a different way. But if that is done with commitment, dedication, and persistence, the chances of the achievements to keep happening are very high. One needs only to look at the history of successful people and organizations. Those capable of reinventing themselves over the years always have a place assured in the podium of the winners.

4

Homework well done

In the corporate world, the "luckiest" people are also those who work the most, prepare the most, dedicate themselves the most, and who endeavor, in body and soul, to achieve their objectives. We are the ones who build our own luck. As a consequence, the results appear. And thus it was with Volvo do Brasil. What we achieved was not by mere chance. It was the outcome of homework well done.

This journey started many years ago with a clearly defined north and well formulated plans that were carefully implemented. We knew where we wanted to be. We knew our strengths and the points to be improved. We created control mechanisms with performance indicators, so that we could correct the route at the slightest sign of deviation.

We counted on the strength of the Volvo Group and on its work tools. In some cases, we used them so well that we became the reference. We adopted with conviction the principle of quantifying, measuring, and delivering. We worked with a view of the integrated and genuinely orchestrated whole. We mapped out the paths and explored all possible synergy. We built a challenging work environment. We dared to test new ideas and different concepts. We stimulated people to give their best, freely and with autonomy.

Brazilians were prepared to take on command positions in replacement of expatriates, who came here for specific periods of time. With more knowledge about the local unit and its operation, they ensured the achievement of objectives under a long-term view.

We had enough courage to make the decisions that were necessary – some were radical and painful. We provided the adequate infrastructure. We offered a reward system that was both compatible and motivating. We created clear policies, with a view to reducing eventual dissatisfaction or comparisons between employees. We placed egos and vanities in their due places.

We adopted a firm posture before Sweden. Our points of view and positions began to be more accepted as we delivered higher results and dividends. The language of money still talks louder and generates more freedom.

However, the turnover moment effectively came when we defined that we wanted to be a world-class company. From then on, we began to adopt metrics and indicators. We wanted to compare our practices to the best ones in existence and to check whether we were walking the talk. In particular, we wanted to verify if what we were doing was aligned with the references of a high-performance company.

The adoption of the Management Excellence Model (MEG), with all the concepts and fundamentals from the National Quality Foundation, was a natural choice. What came next was just work, work, and more work. After having done the homework, we tested our performance with various institutions and different methodologies. And we managed to place Volvo do Brasil in a standout position in the country and in the Volvo Group.

I also had to do my homework to reach where I am in my professional career. Since very early, I had a very clear idea of the world I wanted for myself. And, definitely, it was not the world of my parents. My dream was to go to the big city. I wanted a different life. I was sure that I would overcome the challenges and achieve what I was looking for. After all, no one can choose the point of departure, but everyone can choose the point of arrival.

As young as I was, I had a few years of experience in the corporate world in my baggage and the 3-D that I had learned reading a booklet at a drugstore: dedication, determination, and devotion. What I call today the 3-D view was the key to the achievement of my dreams.

My strategy was clear: first, find a job to be able to eat and not have to run back home. After that, carry on with my studies and go in search of my other objectives. And that's how it happened. The professional experience offset the low level of schooling and I managed to find a job in Curitiba, after having passed by São Paulo and Rio. Following that, the person who had recruited me for that first company went to work for Volvo and hired me again.

During all the phases of my professional career, I worked and worked – as I have always believed I should do. Today, I am proud to be able to say, like my father, that I have never missed a single day of work for lack of willingness. Every morning, I was ready to go to work without any pain in my stomach for the journey that I would have ahead of me. Nothing came for free. Nothing fell into my lap. I only harvested what I planted with lots of dedication, determination, and devotion.

And that's also how it is in sports, another passion that I have in life. Since I wasn't able to practice as a teenager, I now compensate for that with a lot of training and discipline. Sooner or later, the results begin to appear. And they don't come alone. They bring with them a strong feeling of achievement.

In the corporate world, professionals have no other way: if they want to be successful, they must do their best. They have to be aware, however, that their contribution has an expiry date, as life does. While the company follows its path towards continuity on the market, professionals have to face the challenge of planning their careers and the closure of their professional cycle. If they do their homework correctly, they won't fear the future or its challenges. They will know how to choose the best paths and will be able to enjoy post-career life in tranquility. In their hearts, they will have the unmistakable feeling of duty done.

At Volvo do Brasil, we know that the homework is not done just once. It is an ongoing and permanent process that requires discipline. It is not possible to skip stages, much less copy or cheat. It must be done with attention and seriousness, because in today's world there is no space for amateurism. Our commitment is to doing our homework better at each time. We know that results do not happen by chance. They are built step by step, accomplishment by accomplishment.

5

Awareness that life goes on

Life will follow its course, regardless of the results already accomplished. At each moment, new challenges will appear. And the practices and glories of the past will no longer be enough to face them.

We need to be aware that nothing is forever. No one surfs the crest of the wave all the time. That is why we must continue innovating, renovating, and reinventing to be able to remain there as long as possible or, at least, more time than our competitors. We are like a great football player, who must practice and train all the time. He has to be aware that the plays of the past, the weight of the jersey or the tradition of the club, on their own, do not win matches.

At Volvo do Brasil, we know we have come far. We have had many victories and we want more. If we stop striving for excellence in everything we do, we will be easily swallowed up or overtaken. One just needs to look at the history of companies around the world to realize that. For this reason, we have to remain alert and work hard to be one step ahead of the competition with respect to the needs and desires of our customers and other audiences.

I reached the top of the organization early. Many people feel that when this happens life becomes easy and it's possible to relax. With me it was exactly the opposite: that was the moment in which I most demanded of and challenged myself. I knew I would be more required and, therefore, a higher level of dedication would be necessary. I felt I had to continually develop and enhance myself and, at the same time, remain in tune with the evolution of the business, of the company, and of the world. As an effective member of the board, I always tried to go beyond what was expected of me and to look at the organization as a whole.

Even now that I move towards closing the cycle of my professional life, I don't intend to settle down nor be less committed. Much the opposite, I intend to use in corporate life the same strategy that I use in running a marathon. It is in the last kilometers, when exhaustion begins to weigh heavy, that I strive even harder. I gather all my forces and experiences to be able to cross the finishing line with the feeling that I have given my very best and then celebrate the duty done.

It is extremely important to know how to celebrate accomplishments. But we must bear in mind that nothing lasts forever – neither success nor failure. Success can lead to arrogance and, in this sense, it can become an enemy of itself. Preserving humbleness is fundamental. To walk around with your nose in the air can lead to loss of focus and concentration, leading to good sprawls downhill. That's why you must have your feet firmly planted on the ground and focus on what is coming ahead.

Volvo do Brasil is well aware of its dimension and relevance for the Volvo Group. We cannot think that now it is the tail that is going to wag the dog. Alone, we have no life of our own. We are part of a major set of cogwheels. We continue to need the Group's support, strategies, and vision of the future, mainly regarding products. And we are tremendously grateful for all this.

We also need all our business chain to work in a harmonious and integrated way. We depend on the commitment of our suppliers, on the competence of our dealer network, on the loyalty of our customers, and on the professionalism of all our partners. We are like a great chain that, to be truly strong, depends on the strength of each of its links.

Together, we carry on our journey, with the awareness that there is no space for settling back for those who strive permanently for excellence. New challenges will always appear, because life always goes on.

1a e 2a. The first vehicles produced by Volvo in Sweden. **3a.** Morassutti in his Guarda-Mirim uniform when he was an office-boy. **4a.** Employees at the "White House", the first headquarters of Volvo in Curitiba (Morassutti is the first one in the top row, from left to right.) **5a e 6a.** Aerial view of the plant during the construction phase, from 1977 to 1979. **7a e 8a.** Inauguration of the plant by the president of Brazil at that time, João Baptista Figueiredo. **9a.** Current view of the plant.

10a. Morassutti with the former president of Brazil, Luiz Inácio Lula da Silva, in the first Volvo truck produced in the world. **11a e 12a.** Products sold in Brazil. **13a.** Morassutti on the cover of the Brazilian magazine *Você RH* when Volvo do Brasil received the "Best Company to Work for" award in 2008. **14a.** The National Brazilian Quality Award received by Volvo do Brasil in 2009. **15a.** Members of the company board and employees receive the "Best Company to Work for" award in 2011.

PART

II

THE SECRETS OF SUCCESS

6

The heritage received

We have been extremely privileged and benefited by a valuable heritage that we received from the Volvo Group and from Sweden: the Volvo culture. It is comprised of values and principles that consolidated over the course of the Group's history. It has its roots in the good and was forged on practices used with different audiences.

In the treasure chest that we received, we find the Volvo way and the Code of Conduct, which summarize the Volvo Group's business philosophy, values, principles, and corporate culture. They are a true corporate Bible, with accurate guidance that is valid for all the units of the Group anywhere in the world, regardless of the stage of development they are in and of their business practices – obviously, always respecting the local legislation.

Quality, safety, and respect for the environment are core values of the Volvo Group since it was established. Today, other values of equal importance have been added. Besides, the Group adopts energy, passion, and respect for people as a way of working.

In the beginning, even though we were enchanted by this culture, some employees had difficulties in understanding clearly what it meant in practice. We must remember that this happened over three decades ago, at a time when some practices were not common in Brazil like, for example, separating the recyclable garbage. Enthusiastically, we began to do the separation. But, since this was not common in the country, the guys who collected the garbage ended up mixing everything and putting it all in the same bag.

The rule was clear: everyone should wear the seat belt while driving a company's car. And it was followed, but just on the premises. Right after crossing the company's gates, many people released the seat belt, because it was not part of our culture to wear it.

I confess that, initially, I didn't really understand why Volvo would not authorize buying cars in metallic colors for the company pool or for the expatriates. The metallic paint finishing process at the time was harmful to the environment. But in my mind the responsibility for this act belonged to those who manufactured the cars and not to their buyers. I still had not understood the concept of connivance, so clear nowadays.

Working with the concept of quality and safety in an authentic way, giving people freedom and autonomy because they are considered responsible and should know what they are doing, and treating everyone with respect were practices that most of the employees had never seen or experienced before. We started to use a mental model inspired in a nobler concept of doing business, searching for a better work environment, a more humane company, and a more sustainable world.

From being hammered into people for so long, this culture is today strongly rooted in Volvo do Brasil. With a huge power of transformation, it managed to change habits and behaviors. It ended up infecting also the audiences of our relationship, leading to changes in their practices, procedures, and attitudes towards business and life.

This heritage really made the difference, establishing a strong, admired brand in Brazil that is respected and has great credibility. When we look back, we can only thank Sweden and the Volvo Group for this gift.

Likewise, I thank my father for the valuable heritage he gave me. It was not comprised of monetary values or assets, but it was filled with ethical and moral values. My father, even without any schooling, was for me an example of character, conduct, and honesty. He always emphasized the importance of work. I only realized how deeply these values were imbued in me in my adulthood. That was when I realized that they had always guided and sustained my life.

I now understand perfectly my father's behavior and the message he wanted to give me. There is nothing wrong with being a street sweeper, if the work is done in a dignified manner. The merit lies not in the profession itself, but in the way and passion with which it is performed.

The shame I felt in childhood, when I saw him sweeping the streets of the town where we lived, was replaced by the pride of seeing him carefully sweeping the sidewalks and the patio of the Volvo employees' association as an ordinary employee, when I was already a member of the board of Volvo do Brasil.

Sweeping was what he wanted and could do. He did it with a high level of dedication until his death. He didn't have the competencies required to perform other jobs, but he had many moral attributes and used them throughout his life. He believed that he cleaned the world, which in a way can be considered as true. This only increased my admiration for him and encouraged me to practice his teachings.

The heritage that Volvo do Brasil received from the Volvo Group is certainly one of the pillars that has supported our journey. The culture has been a moral compass that guides our conduct and our actions, keeping us as a company of good.

Any company that wants to build a solid success story must have a strong culture based on values. If this culture has deep roots, it will support the organization even in times of storms and will allow its growth to take place in a healthy and consistent way.

7

The mix of cultures

We got to know from up close, admired, and respected the culture and values of the Volvo Group. Over the years, however, we also learned that an adopted culture can work both for good and for bad, if it is not understood correctly.

The valuing of people and the strong belief that they are responsible and reliable are among the Group's principles. Volvo do Brasil incorporated this way of thinking in its policies, in its practices, and in the relationship with the employees since the beginning.

We imported many personnel policies adopted in Sweden and in other countries of the Group and confidently implemented them in Brazil. It was easier than creating new policies. Besides, they had already been successfully tested in other parts of the world. Freedom with responsibility: that was the line of thinking in force.

In the initial stages of the company, employees were hired locally or brought in from other cities. For the roles that required deeper knowledge of the automotive segment, professionals were hired from the state of São Paulo, where the automotive industry was concentrated. Shop floor workers were nearly all hired locally, except for supervisors – at that time called "foremen". Many employees came from the countryside, had a low level of schooling and no link with any union. The idea was exactly to look for people who were far from the strong labor union movement that was taking place in São Paulo. Since they would be trained for their roles here in the plant, no previous experience was required. Almost all leadership positions were occupied by expatriates coming from Sweden.

The contracting routine went ahead at full steam, while the plant was in the final stages of construction. Soon we would move to the Industrial District of Curitiba (CIC), which at that time was a faraway place. "Far from the city" was what we used to say, in particular because we were established in three very central venues: in the famous "white house" on Mateus Leme Street, where I worked, in the office on Comendador Araújo Street, and on Pamphilo de Assunção Street, where a prototype area operated. There was also an office in São Paulo for the Purchasing area.

People continued to arrive in the company, each one with their culture and life story. The professional experience also diverged: there were people from the countryside, from the experienced São Paulo, from large companies, from family businesses, and even from the government. I had come from a Caterpillar dealer – American culture. Previously, I had experienced the culture of a family business.

At the time, the market practice was to control everything at the workplace: photocopies, for which it was even necessary to have a request form signed by the immediate superior, fax messages, telephone calls, office material, clothing etc. The workday was rigid and had to be strictly obeyed. Working overtime was only allowed with previous authorization.

Then, we started to work at Volvo. A culture of freedom: no control over photocopies, free access to the telephone, reinforced snacks, and overtime based on the employee's own discretion. At that time, the company already adopted the flexible working hours concept imported from Sweden: employees were responsible for controlling their own working day and for informing the overtime hours for payment. In short, total freedom for everyone to carry out their activities, mainly in areas that depended more on local actions – as was the case of the administrative area and of HR, where I worked.

We looked at the practices of the Volvo Group and of the local market and offered something even better. In truth, there were few large companies in the region at that time with which we could in fact compare ourselves. At any rate, "at Volvo it has to be better" is what everyone began saying. And everything had to be better: compensation, benefits, and all the other practices and policies.

The quality and variety of food had to be the best of the market. Serving shrimp became something ordinary. Snacks had to be special, both for those who were starting their workday and for those who stayed working overtime. When the bus lines and schedules offered by the company did not address the individual needs, we provided taxis. The health care plan and other benefits did not result in any additional costs for the employees. Even those who had children in public schools received financial support. A true wonder! And at each day the list of concessions only grew.

The demands did not stop and we were not shaken by that. Our objective was to have differentiated policies that would place us in the leading edge. It was the perfect combination: the company wanted to create and offer something different to the employees and they, of course, had the desire to receive a world of different things. So, we ended up having a very nice compensation package, which included excellent benefits, and a work environment visualized only in one's best dreams. The ones who did not really like this were the other companies in the region. Needless to say, the labor union loved it.

The pride of working for Volvo was huge. We wore our name badges and the company shirt even outside work. Our family members used to tell everyone that they had a relative working at Volvo. The children, in particular, bragged at school that their dad worked for Volvo – as if that made him a superhero. The society also began to look at us differently. Since we worked in a multinational, we had status and credit in the community – they even thought we were competent!

In a way, this went to some employees' head. Because of working for a company with such a reputation, they started to believe that they were truly special, superior, and worthy of differentiated treatment. They believed they could cut in line in any establishment and have priority in service at the doctor's office or at the hairdresser. They should receive VIP treatment. The statement "I am from Volvo" should open doors everywhere.

Inevitably, this attitude began to cause adverse reactions. We began to receive countless complaints, from different sources, in terms of the posture of some of our staff and their family members. It was at this moment that we began to realize that we were creating "little monsters". Based on the values of the Volvo Group, we had worked hard to establish a pleasant and differentiated environment in which our employees would be proud to work. And it worked: they were proud. But some of them were excessively proud.

Soon after, the Factory Committee, the entity that represents all the workers, was established. In a way, its appearance was encouraged and facilitated by the company itself, given that in Sweden having this type of representation was normal. I remember well how it all started and I have been a great promoter and defender of this communication channel with the company. However, since the representatives of the committee had free time during working hours to evaluate the internal environment and total freedom to suggest improvements in the capital-labor relation, the sky became the limit in requests and claims.

The taxi had to be special, because common taxis were not safe and this was against the safety principle defended by the company. Lunch had to be increasingly more sophisticated, snacks had to be reinforced, the pool cars had to have more accessories, the parking lot had to be improved, the rooms had to be enhanced, more waiters were needed in the restaurant of the leadership, titles had to be given, positions had to be reviewed. And, of course, the benefits policy needed improvements.

We were experiencing a time of a great welfare drive. A good part of the staff believed that the company should take care of everything for them. Otherwise, it would suffer the injury caused by low productivity and high absenteeism. Social assistance addressed all types of demands and needs. If the employees spent more than their salary, the company would give them a loan. If they did not have money to pay it back, they could get part of their thirteenth salary. Then, they could sell one third of their vacation or get more loans. The creative possibilities to provide support for people were endless. We ended up becoming "mother Volvo".

Initially, we thought that this was for the best of the employees. Later, we realized it was not. Just to give an idea of the size of this, the sum of the charges and the benefits reached approximately 150 percent of the base salary.

As for me, who had come from a very hard world and ended up in the fantastic Volvo world, where everything was offered and provided for, I had absolutely nothing to complain or claim. Much the opposite, while many were asking, I was giving my best. I never struggled for titles, nor did I request a single salary increase in all my professional life. But that did not prevent me from being properly recognized.

My parents were very simple people. And they were very different from each other, in particular in their way of thinking and seeing the world. In common, they shared only a strong belief in work. Together, they complemented each other and gained energy to raise their children and educate them according to their principles.

My mother had acute rheumatoid arthritis since she was a child, but this did not take away from her a huge desire to fight for the things in which she believed. By overcoming the constraints that the disease imposed on her, she became a strong and obstinate person, with a lot of passion for life. She understood that, even against her husband's will, she should fight for her children to study – something she herself had never been able to do – besides working. This would be the only way forward to a better life with less suffering.

She went into battle and created the necessary conditions for this to happen. After managing to get me into the Guarda-Mirim, a local institution program for needy children, she requested authorization from the judge so that I would be allowed to study in the evening, in spite of my young age.

When I told my children that I did my homework by kerosene lamp, they looked at me startled. They didn't even know what a kerosene lamp was. They were also surprised when I told them that electricity reached my house only a long time after. Then I was finally able to buy the first television for the family. And it was a 60. "Inches?", they asked. "Installments," I answered.

Having to watch my mother's struggle to help support her children and at the same time to create the conditions for them to work and study, with the fragile health that she had, caused in me much anguish. At the same time, it was a great inspiration. Somebody healthy and full of life like me had to go into battle. Performing any type of work, and in the best way possible, was the least I could do.

The desire of having things and not being able to buy them, feeling toothache and not being able to afford the dentist, and other hardships that I went through in childhood and adolescence made of me a stronger and more resistant person. I also learned to value each little victory that I achieved along the way, not to waste and, in particular, not to whine on a full belly. Therefore, being on Volvo Fantasy Island was, for me, heaven.

As the demands increased in the company, the motivation decreased, the dissatisfaction appeared, and the spell was broken – not because of the conditions offered, but because of the expectation of a few to quickly reach the top of the organization, to hold an important position, to receive a pompous title and, consequently, to have special advantages.

Practically all the benefits were granted equally across all the levels of the organization. At the time, the travel policy allowed five-star hotels, which could be used by any employee. Even so, some complained and requested special training to learn how to behave in more sophisticated environments. Everyone was entitled to travel business class. Some felt like maharajas. The other benefits were, and continue to be until today, exactly the same for any level.

If there had been the list of best companies to work for at the time, we would certainly have been at the top. But one day all that became unsustainable. The customer did not want to pay more for that and the competition started to become extremely tough.

In addition, we realized that, unfortunately, freedom had been confused with profligacy and was being misused: some employees shared their health care plan with relatives and friends, worked overtime without need just to increase their salaries, used the pool cars to go to the beach, and used the telephone, the photocopiers, and other resources abusively.

It was clear that we had to change, as we had raised some very whiny and pampered children. The taste of deception was bitter. The issue was to find the right moment to make the necessary changes. The moment came practically one decade after the establishment of the company, driven by competitiveness and by the need to reduce costs.

We did what had to be done: we reduced staff through direct dismissals and a voluntary dismissal plan, dried up the structure, reviewed roles and titles, reassessed the benefits whose cost began to be partially shared with the employees, and reformulated the services provided internally – always respecting the current legislation. From "mother Volvo" we became "stepmother Volvo".

Obviously, we destroyed the dreams of many people who had already projected a brilliant future on Fantasy Island. There was a lot of griping. The only reason it wasn't even worse is that the Factory Committee, well aware that the changes were really necessary and would avoid even higher losses, supported the measures adopted.

Many of those who left had difficulties in adapting to other companies – in particular, those who had only worked at Volvo and did not know any other corporate culture. Others, who did not have the courage to leave the company through the voluntary dismissal plan and who lost their roles and titles, started to moan and groan in the corridors. They complained in a veiled way, negatively influencing the internal climate. Today I realize that it would have been healthier for both parties if we had ended their work contracts.

We went through a period of major demotivation among the employees, caused by the loss of conditions that had been offered before. Even the newcomers complained that shrimps were no longer served at lunch, exactly now that they had joined the company.

The reconstruction of the internal environment was necessary and urgent. And it was done step by step, based on the lessons we had learned. We continued to follow the principles of the Volvo Group, which we so admired. However, we adapted the actions to our culture, instead of simply copying what was done in other countries or companies, as their reality was different.

We learned the hard way that nothing can be totally free. Otherwise, people will not value it. The relation with the employees must be respectful and healthy, but also professional and with gains for both parties. Freedom must be earned. Rules, constraints, and penalties are necessary. We must be ahead in terms of concepts and policies, but without losing sight of what is being practiced on the market. We must fly the flag of the company, but within the professional scope and in a responsible way. In short, practices and policies must be adjusted to the stage in which the organization finds itself. The leading edge has a price and, at times, it is too high.

With this learning, we grew, matured, and managed to build the culture of Volvo do Brasil: a mix of the Brazilian culture and of the Volvo Group's. With our own culture adapted to our reality, we started to believe more in our capacity. And we moved on.

8

Common north – shared vision

We have never hidden from the employees Volvo do Brasil's business plans and ambitions. The North to be followed and the objectives to be achieved have always been presented in a clear and transparent way. We believe that everyone in our organization has to have the correct map in hands, in order not to spend energy going down mistaken paths that will not lead to the expected destination. The departure and the arrival points must be clearly outlined.

In the past, due to the way we were structured and to the smaller number of workers, we would hold meetings in the Viking Association sports gymnasium, on the premises, to disclose the organization's business plan to everyone. Musical, theater, or dance performances, outcomes of cultural projects sponsored by us, always gave a special color to the event.

More recently, given the large number of people involved and the current organizational structure, each business area holds its own event. In addition to the specific business plan of the area, the overarching plan of the organization is also shown. The vision of the whole, the synergy among the areas, and the importance of working together are strongly emphasized.

Aligning all the actions is fundamental not to lose focus. Everyone in the organization must look to the same north and move in its direction, committed and decided to achieve a common purpose.

The North to be followed is established by the Volvo Group's vision and by the local objectives and challenges. In the near future, we will have a different methodology to define global objectives. Currently, however, the starting point for the establishment of the business plans is the challenge letters that the Volvo Group sends annually to all business areas. These must carefully evaluate the challenge that is being proposed and respond if they accept it or not, giving the appropriate justifications. Based on this, the business plans are drafted, driven by the principle of sustainable growth, product lifecycle management, and operational excellence.

Each business area disseminates its respective business plan to its staff. These objectives are later broken down into targets for the divisions and departments until they reach the individual level. At this point, they become part of the Personal Business Plan of each employee.

The objectives of each employee, department, division, business area, as well as the corporate ones, are included in everyone's Profit Sharing Plan, in different blocks. It is a way to have everyone mobilized for the blocks of objectives to be achieved in their entirety, as this will have a direct impact on the amount of profit share to be paid to each individual. The company wins and so do the employees. That's fair enough.

Among the corporate objectives that are valid for the entire organization, I highlight two of major importance: the financial results and the outcome of the assessment of the corporate management excellence level. This evaluation can be undertaken by independent auditors or by the National Quality Foundation (FNQ), given that we deploy this entity's excellence criteria and, every time we are candidates to the National Brazilian Quality Award (PNQ), we are evaluated by them.

For this process to work, we need to mobilize the entire company. There are thousands of employees in a wide range of vastly different functions and we must make sure that each one does their share. Everyone has to be truly committed and work with a high level of passion for the whole to operate adequately and to make sense.

In personal life, the process should be no different. Each individual should clearly define what they want from life and formulate plans to get there – or, at least, to have an idea of the path to be followed. Without having a defined north, life is left to the winds. And, at times, these may blow in the wrong direction.

We are the ones who build our own future. We must fight for what we really want. We must take command of our lives, instead of placing ourselves as victims of fate. I have always had a clear north to follow and fought for the things I defined in my life plan – fully aware that there is always a price to be paid or something to be given up. The price often means having to go beyond exhaustion, because that far the majority goes. In the marathons and long distance bicycle competitions in which I participate, I have noticed that the number of people at the starting line is high. But the number of people that effectively cross the finishing line is much lower. I don't give up easily. I learned that, in any job or sports activity, what carries people forward is mental power – much more than physical fitness, skills, or competencies.

Accomplishing dreams can never be delegated. This responsibility is far too heavy to place on the shoulders of family members, friends, or company. Each individual must personally go after their dreams, walk each step of the journey, learn with each curve on the way, and keep on going – always in tune with the larger plan of existence over which we have no control. But what depends on us only we can do.

At Volvo do Brasil, we will continue communicating, with a high level of clarity and transparency, our plans and ambitions. We want all employees to have a clear vision of the North to be followed. We believe in the power of this vision as motivation for everyone to join the same cause. Sharing generates commitment and involvement. And that's all we are looking for.

When thousands of workers, mobilized by the same vision, roll up their sleeves and carry on in the same direction, everything becomes possible – even those dreams that seem further away.

9

The quest for excellence

It seemed to be unachievable – until the day we took the first steps. From then on, we walked with firm and consistent strides. And, finally, we reached the target: we achieved the threshold of "world-class company", as a consequence of the National Brazilian Quality Award (PNQ), which we were awarded by the National Quality Foundation (FNQ).

To become part of the select group of companies that have won this award is something extremely gratifying, which will forever remain in the history of Volvo do Brasil and in the records of the FNQ. For us, it was a confirmation of our high performance and excellence in management. We had already felt this through the pride of our employees and of the Volvo Group with respect to our practices. But having this validated by an institution of renown, which has a high level of local and international credibility, made us feel tremendously honored.

When the winning companies were announced, I felt butterflies in my stomach. First, for the emotion of victory. After that, because I saw in my mind the film of how it had all begun. I even remembered the day in which we had a board meeting to decide whether or not we would be candidates to the PNQ. We were going through one of those moments when possible measures for cost reduction are on the table. When it was mentioned that if we received the award we would have expenses with internal events and would have to contribute with an amount to the award ceremony, the decision was made not to participate. The argument was that we had to be coherent with the cost reduction message that we were sending out to the organization. And that, of course, made sense.

Even so, I was disappointed. I mentally reviewed all the work done in the organization for so many years in the quest for excellence. In the previous year, we had been the standout in the Processes category. In the thank you speech in São Paulo, I affirmed that in the next year we would be there to receive the 2009 PNQ. And exactly now, when I was sure of our victory, the decision was made not to participate. For me, it made no sense not to candidate the company for the award after so much effort and preparation. In spite of not having the award itself as the final objective, I had never hidden my desire of seeing Volvo receive it.

Unable to comply with that, I said in an impulse that, if the problem were the costs, I would find a sponsor in the community willing to encourage competitiveness and the quest for excellence in companies. With this promise, our candidacy ended up being approved. Anyway, if we did not make the decision right then and there, we would not have time to register our application.

A few months later, we received the coveted award. And finding a sponsor was not even needed. The company was already at a more favorable moment and the board understood that this would no longer be necessary.

The award ceremony was held in high style and was attended by a number of authorities and entities that always honor this event. Euphoric, we celebrated the results with our staff, thanking everyone for the excellent work they had been doing for so many consecutive years.

The journey for excellence effectively changed the history of Volvo do Brasil, placing the company at another level. As we progressed in actions, the leaps in performance levels were visible. Attested by independent auditors, they were translated into numbers and points won in the metric scale of the PNQ. The systemic view allowed us to see the whole and to perceive the interdependence among the different audiences. This way, the company became more and more sustainable.

I remember quite well the first evaluations we performed to discover our position with respect to the existing best practices. We based ourselves on the concepts and criteria of the Malcolm Baldrige National Quality Award, used in the United States to evaluate the level of excellence of organizations. We achieved approximately 350 points on a scale of 1,000 points. We were far below the necessary score to be a world-class company. This was in the late 1990s.

But we wanted to get there. We rolled up our sleeves and began working hard to increase our level of excellence. We knew it would not be easy to move out of the 350 points and double the score to reach the threshold we desired. We had in our favor a history marked by commitment to quality. Quality is in our DNA. It runs in our veins, processes, and products. We had already been deploying several other management practices such as Operational Development (OD), World-class Manufacturing (WCM), Volvo Industrial System (VIS), and others. It was just a matter of consolidating all the work that was already being done.

I had acted as a facilitator in a Juran quality program in the 1980s and understood quite well the importance of having indicators to measure quality and its progress. I had remained involved with the topic since then and liked the idea of striving for excellence. What we would have to do was basically jump from "quality management" to "excellence in management".

The board embraced the cause. It gave us unconditional support to all the work that would have to be done. We adopted the Management Excellence Model (MEG) of FNQ, the entity that manages the PNQ in

Brazilian territory. This model deploys a systemic view of the organizational management and is comparable to the excellence model applied by the European Foundation for Quality Management (EFQM) in Europe, by the Deming Prize in Japan, and by the previously mentioned Malcolm Baldrige National Quality Award (MBNQA).

The MEG, totally aligned with Volvo's values, is driven to the future and to sustainability. The model helps companies to develop effective management and governance tools, with a view to increasing the competitiveness of organizations and of Brazil.

Councils and sub councils were established at Volvo do Brasil to deal with the main topics related to excellence. All the company areas were involved. The quest for excellence became a priority. In order to encourage performance even further at all levels of the organization, the result of the assessment of the company's excellence level became part of the Profit Sharing Plan. This way, all employees started to monitor this item, since it had direct repercussion in their pockets.

The strategy worked: we received the award. As a winning company, we have to stay out of the selection process for two years. After that, we will apply again. We feel that our processes are increasingly more consistent and aligned with the MEG. We have also realized that the journey for excellence is endless. We will always be striving for the best practices and concepts, trying to achieve higher levels of performance. This has already become part of our culture.

We have recently established the Innovation Council, with a view to consolidating the culture of innovation and preserving the environment of knowledge generation that we have. Among other actions, the council established the Volvo Innovation Award. Employees from any area and of any level can apply, individually or in teams, by submitting innovative practices that can effectively be implemented and bring about results for the organization. This prize was inspired in the Bank of Ideas that we had in the past and in the I9 (Innovate) Program that currently recognizes the best ideas in the manufacturing area. In addition, one of the targets established for the Profit Sharing Plan of the industrial workers is the suggestion of ideas.

We compare the journey for excellence to going up an escalator that moves downwards. The effort to go up the steps is high. On the other hand, the simple fact of standing still takes you down and makes you lose points. The challenge is huge, but even so we have moved forward. While we wait for the moment when we will be allowed to apply for the award again, we carry on working with the excellence model and undergoing independent audits. According to these appraisals, we have managed to improve our score even further, which maintains us in the threshold of world-class companies.

I believe that the fundamentals and concepts of the excellence model can also be applied to one's personal life. In the same way that the company must have a systemic view that addresses the entire business chain, individuals must have a wide-ranging view that comprises all dimensions of life. Somcone's success cannot be measured only by the career or by the assets built. Having a broader life plan is fundamental. Adjustments will always be necessary, given that there are many variables and that some of them are not under our control. But this is no reason not to formulate a plan.

I have seen many professionals who dedicate themselves body and soul to work – only to work. They have no other interest in life. They put family in second place, have no time for friends, do not perform any kind of physical activity, have no idea of what leisure is. They are reluctant to go out on vacation. When they do, they do not manage to switch off their computers or cell phones. As they have a worldview that is totally focused on work, these people will face huge difficulties to disconnect from the company at their retirement. They will have the feeling that life is over. In reality, they will only be closing one of the cycles in life: the professional one.

Other cycles, equally important, will be just beginning. All it will take is a focus adjustment. With less pressure and stress, there will be more time for people to take care of themselves, to be with the ones they love, to carry out interesting activities, to learn new things, to put in practice dormant talents, to accomplish dreams that were left behind.

Work is very important. But, certainly, it is not the sole important thing. A balanced life is much healthier and brings much more happiness – not only for the individuals but also for their families, their friends, and the company they work for. Balanced and happy people have more energy to carry out activities, are more creative, face challenges with more tranquility, relate better to others, and, bottom line, end up becoming better professionals.

The quest for excellence must also be ongoing in our personal lives. It is necessary to observe what is not working well, analyze what needs to be improved, and formulate targets to get there. At the same time, we have to maintain and reinforce the areas that are already flowing well and that will provide support for our journey. Taking on the role of manager of our own lives is fundamental for things to happen in a harmonious and sustainable way.

When someone or a company reaches a level of excellence, everyone around receives the benefits and is boosted to follow in the same direction. Likewise, when a light is turned on, it lights up everything that is around it and serves as a guide for those who are in darkness.

Volvo do Brasil has become a reference in the corporate world. And the ongoing quest for excellence was certainly a decisive factor for this to happen. It was a true watershed. The level of maturity that we achieved as an organization, the knowledge we acquired, and the results we delivered attest to the fact that going down the trails of excellence is worthwhile – and very much so.

10

The VdB condominium

I always say: Volvo do Brasil has to be greater and better than the sum of the Business Areas and Units. And so it has been. The "condominium" model made us stronger and is today our biggest differential in the Volvo world.

Volvo do Brasil is like a mini Sweden. Here, all Volvo operations, which in Sweden are established in different cities, are located within the same industrial complex – only in different buildings.

You can easily take a tour of the Volvo world in our campus. You can start by the engine and gearbox plant and then walk over to the cab plant. On the way back, you can visit the truck and bus assembly lines. Walking a little further, you will see the test track and you can hold a test drive on the track for customers. You can then visit the construction equipment demo center and the vehicle delivery center which are right close by. A few more steps and you will reach the place where the new global parts distribution center will be built.

Then, you can visit the commercial areas of construction equipment, marine engines, trucks, and buses. After that, you can visit the Volvo bank and walk over to the different technical and support areas by following the signs.

If it is a nice day, you can extend the walk all the way to the Viking Association – the employees' club – that includes football pitches, tennis courts, sports gymnasium, fitness center, barbecue pits, and a large green area. Then you can follow the ecological trail, breathing in the pure air of the preserved forest, and reach the Volvo Environmental Center. During the visit, it is worthwhile talking to the community people who participate in the courses and activities offered there. On the way back, you can stop for coffee at the Citizenship Street, located in the middle of the plant, where different services are available to the staff.

If you are not short of breath and still in the mood, there are many more interesting things to see. The campus occupies a total area of 1.3 million square meters, with a built area of over 100,000 square meters and capacity to produce over 30,000 vehicles a year. We are one of the largest industrial complexes of the Volvo Group and the only one that has all the operations in one site.

The Volvo do Brasil legal entity comprises all the businesses of the Group in Latin America. In addition to tax and legal issues, we are responsible for the consolidation of results and information regarding these businesses and for their disclosure to the external audiences. The legal entity is managed by a statutory board that historically has been composed of six or seven members.

Since the company was founded, we have worked hard for it not to be perceived in a segmented way, but rather as a single organization. We wanted the employees to feel that they belonged to Volvo do Brasil and not to the specific area in which they worked: buses, trucks, industrial, or commercial. We were a single team. We all worked together – literally. Quite often, areas were separated from each other just by a screen or by the walls of a building. The company was led by a president, to whom all areas reported. The command line was clearly established through a hierarchical structure.

And so it worked for many years. In the late 1990s, though, the president of the company told me he had the feeling that the axis of decision would be modified and that he would be the last president with real power over the entire organization. And he was right: some time later the Volvo Group started to have a matrix structure, divided into Business Areas and Business Units.

This way, instead of having the president reporting to Sweden on all the operations of Volvo do Brasil, we started to have executives reporting directly to a boss abroad and no longer to the local president.

The figure of Volvo do Brasil legal entity's president continued to exist, but as responsible for the joint company and as the spokesperson for the local organization and for the other businesses of the Group in Latin America. For this role, the head office has appointed the main executive in the Trucks division, as this division is the one with the highest economic relevance in Brazil. He is no longer responsible for the operational results of each business, though. He accounts only for the operational results of Trucks.

It was in this new context that the concept of "corporate condominium" appeared. Since we were all in the same physical space, it would not make sense for each Business Area or Unit to start making decisions and hiring services to provide needs that were common to all the others. If we continued treating internal and external corporate issues collectively, we would have gains of scale and would benefit hugely from the synergy.

And so we did. The "condominium" manages the services that are used by all areas – from the simplest to the most strategic ones. It is also responsible for the corporate policies that are valid for the entire organization. Issues related to the external audience are equally treated corporately.

Thus, the person responsible for each Business Area or Unit accounts globally for the final result of their operation, but not for the corporate issues. These are defined and approved by the local Volvo do Brasil board.

With clearly defined coexistence rules and the symbolic figure of the "condominium manager" to maintain order and preserve corporate practices and policies, we have harvested great results. Everyone realized the importance of being together and of adding efforts for the common good. This way we managed to prevent the different Business Areas or Units from doing things in duplicity, from building their own castles, and from starting to compete with each other – as it is common in the corporate world.

It was only sometime later, when the concept of "corporate condominium" had already been incorporated at Volvo do Brasil, that we received the first global guidelines for joint companies. Since we were already experiencing this concept in practice, we became a benchmark for other industrial complexes of the Group.

The global structure, however, is not always aligned with this concept. Each Business Area or Unit has a solid organization, with its own rules and guidelines that must be followed by all its subsidiaries throughout the world. But when the demand from one of them comes to Brazil, it sometimes conflicts with the requests presented by the others or with the internal rules of our "condominium". And harmonizing all this in the best way possible is not always an easy task.

Several times I had to explain to global leaders that the title or benefit that they would like to grant a local executive was not recommended, according to the rules of our "condominium". For those who have never experienced this concept in real life, it can be quite hard to understand that at a first moment. On the other hand, the opposite also happens: when we realize that a global request from a specific area can contribute to the local business, we implement it in the "condominium" as a whole.

The local board has always been a great believer in the benefits of the "corporate condominium" and has been consistent and firm in its decisions. We work hard to maintain a functional, synergistic, and lean structure. As far as possible, we avoid duplicating controls and functions and increasing the internal costs. These would add no value to the business and would end up having to be passed on to the final product.

As one of the representatives of the Volvo do Brasil legal entity for many years, with all that this implies, I have always tried to take care of the interests of the company as a whole. I don't consider myself responsible only for my area. Subconsciously or not, I ended up incorporating the role of "condominium manager". I work hard for all Business Areas and Units to receive the support they need and, at the same time, to be aligned with the corporate guidelines and values.

When people realize that the intention is serious, well-founded, and targets at the highest good of the organization, it is not necessary to have formal power to get things done. All it takes is the moral power. This was the greatest learning that I had over the course of all these years. I have defended countless issues before my board colleagues and other executives with greater power than my own. They could simply tell me to mind my own business, but they don't. They always respect me and give support in the decisions, because they know I am defending the interests of the company as a whole. Many have actually waived a personal position or a spot opinion in favor of the highest good of the organization in the long term.

As I truly believe in the "condominium" concept, I am very attentive for the decisions made to be respected by everyone. But, to have credibility, I have to set the example. It is no use requiring that leaders of other areas think about the highest good of the organization, if I don't do that when I make decisions in my own area. On the other hand, I feel rewarded when I realize that everything works in an integrated manner. And, as I walk around the campus, it is a pleasure to see that many of the enhancements that I have supported – from a simple garden to a new building – have been implemented.

I always work looking at the whole. I carefully analyze the impact on all the parties involved before taking any decisions. I do this not only at Volvo but also in the other entities where I act: Vikingprev (the employees'pension fund), Viking Association, Solidarity Foundation, National Association of Automotive Vehicle Manufacturers (Anfavea), and others. In all these associations and councils, I have always defended the sustainable management, under a long-term view.

I strongly believe in the strength of the whole. Together, we will always be stronger. And so it has been at Volvo do Brasil. The concept of "corporate condominium" has made us a more solid and cohesive company. All areas have benefited from it. But the greatest benefit was certainly for the customers and, consequently, for the Volvo Group and its shareholders.

Our objective is to make everyone realize that we are a "condominium" in Brazil and feel the gains afforded by this model. In this task, we count on the support from the top leaders of the Volvo Group, who have always emphasized that we all need to work in a synergistic and lean way, and with the vision of the whole.

Living in harmony in a "corporate condominium" is an art form. It requires ability, competence, tolerance, and lots of patience. But the result is rewarding. Synergy brings visible and tangible gains – and proves that the whole is greater than the sum of the parts.

11

Strategic partners

"Tell me who you go with and I'll tell you who you are." Volvo do Brasil has always strived to ally itself with good people. We have chosen our partners not only for their technical competencies or for commercial reasons. Above all, we have chosen them for their ethical conduct and professional posture. We look for people who deliver on their word and have the same values as ours.

It has been like that since the beginning. The establishment of the Volvo plant in Curitiba had the strategic support of the local government and other authorities. They all perceived that the project would drive the industrial development of the city and that it would mean a major step towards modernity.

People always ask me about the tax benefits that we received back then. I explain that they were exclusively those established in the current legislation at the time. They are not even comparable to the benefits that started to be granted to new companies years later, when the tax war was established in the country for the purpose of attracting new investments.

The relationship of trust and partnership that we established with the government and other authorities has remained solid over the years and lasts until today. We can say that they were our first strategic partners on Brazilian soil.

Some entrepreneurs from the state of Paraná, together with the Paraná Development Bank S.A. (Badep), were also important partners in the initial establishment of the company. Later on, Volvo bought their shares.

We counted equally on our Swedish partners who, in their vast majority, always believed in and supported this enterprise – beginning by the shareholders, who invested their money on the project.

The partnership with the local community began together with the first steps taken by Volvo in Curitiba. It gained strength in the plant construction phase, when a number of different companies had to be contracted. To date, I still find people who speak with pride of having helped to raise the walls of the plant, where there was nothing but a plantation of tomatoes. They keep great memories of this venture.

Following that, hundreds of other partners came along. With their services and products, they have supported the company and have contributed to its success. They all cheer and celebrate every achievement that we accomplish as if the company were theirs. And in truth it is. They are all part of the Volvo world: the team that keeps our workplace clean and pleasant, the security guards that protect us 24 hours a day, the people who carefully prepare thousands of meals every day, the people who beautify our gardens, the photographers and film crews who record our best moments. We have countless professionals from small and large companies at our side every day, making our workday feasible and easier.

We also count on a solid base of suppliers of parts and components for production. Some of these companies are even larger than we are. We find in them serious and committed partners that, with a high level of competence, supply our assembly lines. The majority is still located in the state of São Paulo. Some are located in Minas Gerais and a few in Paraná. The so much desired strong supplier base in Paraná unfortunately has not progressed as we wished it had. This is an item that remains pending and requires more structured actions. Even so, it is undeniable that there have been major advances in the development of suppliers in the region.

Practically all non-production items such as equipment, materials, and services for the support areas are acquired here in Curitiba, from reliable partners that produce and deliver with quality.

Renowned educational institutions and highly qualified professionals, in the area of human and organizational development, have also been valuable partners. They have been with us at each step of the journey towards excellence. They have contributed hugely not only to the development of the company but also to the personal growth of our staff.

Companies from the third sector have counseled us, with competence and sensitivity, in issues involving diversity and inclusion, endeavoring to provide disadvantaged young people and disabled people with a new chance in life.

In-house, we have dedicated partners: our employees. Day after day, they undertake their work with competence, professionalism, and passion. They know they need to do their part well for the whole to operate adequately.

At the other end, as an extension of our plant, there are the dealers that sell our products to the final customers. We have a very competent network, with houses spread throughout Brazil and in other countries of Latin America. Some are long-standing partners that have been with Volvo do Brasil since it was established, both in moments of prosperity and in those that were not so favorable. They know our products and customers like no one else. Many actually say that the Volvo blood runs in their veins. They are strong groups that individually sell more in a year than it is sold in several countries where the Volvo Group operates.

Respect, trust, and open dialogue have always been the basis of our relationship with our dealers. So much so that this relationship ended up becoming a reference for the Volvo world – not only for the results achieved but also for the practices adopted.

We also have a solid partnership with our importers located in Latin America. In spite of the inherent difficulties in trading with some countries, we carry on together and with confidence.

Finally, we have our major partner. The one that is the reason for our existence and that effectively supports the entire business chain: our customer, who trusts in our brand and carries on buying our products. He admires the beautiful design and sophisticated technology, values comfort and safety, sees the quality stamped in every detail, perceives the concern with the environment, and feels in his pocket the benefits brought by the competitiveness of our products. It is for him that we work with extreme dedication. We want to be increasingly more deserving of his trust, not only in our products but also in the company as a whole. This is our major commitment.

Volvo do Brasil has always chosen its partners carefully, so that the competencies can complement each other and build a successful chain. We understand that a chain is only strong when all the links are made of the same raw material, when everything fits in harmony and moves in the same direction.

We know that being a partner of ours is not easy. We are demanding. We want high-quality products and services. We look for innovative and sustainable solutions. We chase for the deadlines that were agreed and the word that was given – in the same way that we honor ours. We demand commitment, loyalty, ethics, and compliance with all legal aspects. That is, we extend to our partners the same level of demand that we have internally.

Constantly challenged to give their best and encouraged to go further, our partners often end up going beyond their own limits to service us. This way, they develop and grow. Many times we also learn with them. And we carry on, side by side, like good old partners.

When I left home to try to make it in the city, my mother hugged me and said:

– Son, there are two ways of achieving success in life. The first one is being intelligent. The second one is surrounding yourself with competent people.

I was about to thank her for the advice when she added:

– In your case, son, make sure you surround yourself with competent people.

Joking apart, that's what I have tried to do along my professional life: to surround myself with competent people, who are willing to go beyond expectations – people who go into battle and make things happen. And the results have been fantastic.

I have also learned that it's not enough to be with people. We must establish bonds. We spend most part of our lives at work. Establishing relationships based on trust, friendship, and respect is fundamental and extremely healthy. It generates learning and drives our development and evolution.

We can learn with everything and from everyone. The boy who waters the plants in the company one day walked into my office and found me seriously focused on some papers. Instead of talking about football, like he normally did, he asked me if there was a problem. I raised my head and sighed:

– It's all askew...

To which he answered without even blinking:

– Askew doesn't mean it's wrong. Fishing hooks are askew and they're right.

With a laugh, he walked out of my office after wishing me a good day.

I stood still, thinking about those words said so spontaneously. All of a sudden, I started to look at what I was doing from another angle and realized the boy was right: askew is not necessarily wrong.

We can always learn from people, even from those who apparently would have nothing to teach us. We must only be open and receptive. Likewise, it is also important to share what we have learned. If learning is kept under lock and key, it will lose force and usefulness as times goes by. But if it is shared with others, it will remain alive – will be updated and enhanced. It doesn't matter who sowed the seed. The important thing is that the tree grows and bears good fruits. Everyone will benefit.

The partner companies form with us a great team, forged by the team spirit and by the awareness that together we are stronger. They know that they don't work for Volvo, but *with* Volvo. And that makes all the difference.

12

The power of engagement

To have a highly inspiring and motivating environment, where people feel respected, valued, and heard, has always been one of our main priorities. In order to create an environment like this, we have established with our employees a relationship based on much dialogue and transparency. The result has been extremely rewarding: the vast majority is satisfied, committed, and truly engaged.

The high level of engagement appears clearly in the organizational climate survey, named Volvo Group Attitude Survey, that is undertaken simultaneously in every unit of the Volvo Group once a year. The survey evaluates the level of satisfaction of the staff regarding different aspects: leadership styles, relationship, communication, ethical behavior, professional perspectives, and even work facilities and equipment. Volvo do Brasil's indices of satisfaction, pride, and engagement are always among the highest of the Group.

The evaluations undertaken by different institutions from outside the Volvo world also attest to these indices. As a consequence of that, we have received countless awards as the best company to work for in the state of Paraná, in the South region, and in Brazil. Pride and engagement always appear as standout points.

The way we treat our employees does not reflect only in the results of different surveys, but also in other performance indicators. Above all, it is appreciated and recognized by the very people who work with us, given that they are the ones whose opinion about the company is asked and who indicate their level of engagement.

And that's how it has been since the beginning. When we started to manufacture the first vehicles in Curitiba, the Brazilians who had been hired had to undergo an intense learning period in an environment that was totally new, but highly motivating. At every moment, the Swedes showed their total trust in people and in their achievement potential. People paid back with commitment and much willingness to make things happen.

We started our journey with few employees. Today, there are thousands of them. In all these years, passion and engagement have always been present. These ingredients make the majority remain with us, even when harassed by other companies. In general, offers of titles and higher salaries are just not enough. The Volvo way that is characterized by the organization's culture, the environment, the relationship with people, the working conditions, and the trust and commitment to the future of the company end up speaking louder in the moment of decision.

The special events for employees who celebrate 10 and 25 years in the company are always marked by lots of emotion, in particular the one for those who are celebrating 25 years of service, which is also attended by family members. Usually, we project pictures of the employees, in addition to images and striking facts that happened during that period in the company and around the world. And then we can clearly see the changes. Starting by people's faces: those young men and women who were taking their first steps in their professional lives – filled with hope, expectations, and dreams – have become mature and satisfied professionals, with many stories to tell. They carry in their eyes the joy of those who did their best and delivered, with a high level of competence, what they were supposed to. In their hearts they carry a huge pride for the company that they helped to build and in which they are leaving their mark.

They have now a solid record of personal and professional accomplishments – among them, the one of remaining in the company for 25 years. At the award ceremony, it becomes clear to me that they would not be there if they were not committed and deeply engaged people. I have the same certainty when I talk to people who are about to retire, after a whole life almost totally dedicated to the company.

It all becomes easier when you have a passion for the things you do. The motivation that makes me get up earlier to practice for a sports event is the same one that makes me wake up and go to work. It makes me dive headfirst, channel my energy, and persevere in my purpose, without anyone having to remind me of what needs to be done. When the choice is conscious, engagement follows naturally.

Very often, the price to achieve a target is high. Along the way, we will face some stages that are not so pleasant, but they are necessary. In addition to being part of the learning and of the maturation process, they serve to test our level of determination and obstinacy.

Many people behave like fire on straw. They start something very thrilled, as if it were the best thing in the world. At the first sign of difficulty, however, they lose interest and motivation. They begin to see defects in everything and everyone. For them, the entire world is wrong. But, in reality, the outer world is only a reflection of themselves and of their beliefs.

They easily point out the guilty parties for their dissatisfaction: their boss is demanding and lacks vision, their friends do not cooperate, their family does not support them, their financial situation is not favorable etc. And they quickly start looking for something else.

They never stay long enough to untie the knots and learn the lessons. They give up easily. They do not make any additional effort to improve the situation and do not pay the necessary price to achieve what they desire.

From my standpoint, these people would have to look at themselves and work out some internal issues before moving on. Otherwise, the story will repeat itself indefinitely. The scenarios will be different, but the main character will always be the same and will continue to carry inside the same old conflicts.

In the work environment, many times I have noticed that people's greatest difficulty is interacting with others and establishing links. They are so focused on themselves and so deeply immersed in their own world that they cannot see the other people. They cannot perceive what is going on around them. They do not engage themselves. They remain at the margin of the process. And, what is even sadder, they stay miles away from happiness.

I usually say that people are hired for their technical competency and fired for their "lack of competency" in relationships. Even the best experts in a certain field will not last long inside any company if they are impossible to coexist with. If they do not leave on their own advice, the environment will find a way to expel them.

Becoming engaged is fundamental. We need to move out of ourselves and take part in something bigger which transcends the walls of the individual "me". We need to help build, to feel part of, to commit to. This may be the key to the dream of self-achievement that we all strive so hard to accomplish.

At Volvo do Brasil, engagement is clearly visible and widely known. It translates itself into motivation, performance, commitment, and pride of being part of our organization. It is stamped not only in the statistics and the results, but mainly in people's smile. One just needs to walk around the production and other areas of the company to perceive that.

Engagement does not happen overnight. In our case, it was built through a solid relation of respect and trust that we have established with our employees since the very beginning and that has translated into consistent and long-lasting policies. Much more than a factor in competitiveness, engagement is today a rich treasure that we want to preserve, as we are fully aware of its value.

13

Commitment to a better world

An organization that strives for excellence in everything it does must have an encompassing view that crosses its own boundaries and reaches beyond its own navel. It must see the world around and contribute to making it better and more sustainable. It must take concrete actions that can promote the development of the society. Not as a self-promotion or marketing ploy, but as a socially responsible company that knows it can make the difference – and does, through authentic and consistent programs.

As a company, we cannot stop addressing the demands and needs of the world of today. But we have the firm conviction that we can do this without compromising the world of tomorrow. We have never hidden that we want and must make money to sustain our business and the entire chain. However, this can be done with responsibility, with ethics, and with a look that goes beyond the purely financial aspects.

In order to grow, we need to align our past, present, and future, having the values in which we believe as a basis. Since the establishment of Volvo do Brasil, our actions have been guided by strong ethical and moral principles, targeting at a sustainable world and at gains for all parties involved.

The Volvo Group has always emphasized that all its companies must, at least, comply with the legislation and the legal obligations of the country where they are located. And, whenever possible, they should go a bit further. Volvo wants to be admired and respected not only for the quality of its products and services but also for the socially responsible behavior that is characteristic of a citizen company. To this end, it has always adopted a proactive posture with respect to the concerns of the world of today and of tomorrow. It is fully aware that we are part of the problem, but also of the solution.

I began to understand a bit better the extent of Volvo's commitment to a sustainable world when I saw the topic "environment" on the agenda for a leadership development program in Sweden, in which I participated back in the 1980s. We even had a practical class: a picnic by the edge of a highway, with snow falling directly on our heads, for the purpose of evaluating the effect of emissions from vehicles on the environment. Our task was to analyze the bark of the trees, comparing the side that faced the highway with the side that faced the forest, to check the damage caused by pollution.

With my brain nearly frozen, I found that very odd. At that time, countless trees were cut down in Brazil every day and no one was worried about the consequences. Ecological awareness only began to be developed in our country years later and, even so, regrettably many trees continued to be felled.

The work on the highway, which had the support from specialists of renowned institutions and from Volvo technicians, made us realize the impact that the vehicles manufactured by the Group had on nature. It also showed us the deep concern that the company had in finding solutions for this type of issue. Following that, a number of alternatives to reduce emissions and their impacts, which were already under study, were gradually implemented in our vehicles.

Another fact that drew my attention in Sweden was that it is allowed to stroll in private properties located in forest regions. People can even eat the wild fruits that they find on the way without any problems. They just have to keep a certain distance from the houses in order not to invade the privacy of people. That is, they can freely enjoy nature, without owning anything.

Over the years, I was able to realize that quality, safety, and respect for the environment weren't just part of Volvo's discourse. The products developed really had these values as a basic assumption. Furthermore, the Volvo Group is a signatory of the United Nations Global Compact since 2001.

In the industrial processes that we have in Brazil, we monitor continually, through countless indicators, the level of energy used, the consumption of water, the content of gases issued, the noise level, the selective disposal of waste, and all the other impacts that can be caused on the environment. We constantly encourage the intelligent and conscious use of natural resources.

Social responsibility actions have also started early – and in-house. Our employees were the first ones to benefit from a number of programs that we implemented internally. Among these, a literacy course, followed by completion of basic education, and more recently digital inclusion. Lessons in citizenship were provided through voluntary service programs, collection of donations, establishment of the Volvo blood bank, and so many other actions promoted by the company, which encourage our employees to engage in social and environmental causes.

The involvement with the community's social problems started a long time ago. One of the concrete actions in this sense was the establishment of the Solidarity Foundation in 1989, which is maintained by contributions from the employees and from the company. The entity fosters, in shelter homes, close to sixty children in situations of risk and abandonment and gives them the chance of a new life, through educational, recreational, and cultural activities. In over twenty years of existence, the Foundation has helped to rescue countless children and to form many citizens.

The Viking Association cedes the use of its facilities and promotes a number of social practices targeted at the community in the surroundings of the plant. The Capoeira and Citizenship Project and a number of different sports activities help to build the self-esteem of dozens of children and teenagers. The Athlete of the Future Program, in partnership with the Social Service for Industry (Sesi), offers sports and cultural activities in the school off-shift, with a view to developing citizenship.

The Volvo Environmental Center, established in 2007, is located in the plant premises amid a wood of preserved native vegetation. It is intended for cultural, leisure, and research projects, focused on environmental preservation and on the development of ecological awareness. The center takes countless actions aimed at developing the nearby community such as theatre activities for children that approach citizenship and ecology issues; sewing workshops; special make-up and hairdo courses for performances; and application of prints on T-shirts. Many people who take part in these workshops find later a position on the market thanks to the qualification acquired.

Volvo has always encouraged diversity in the workplace in broad terms, promoting actions that go far beyond the legal requirements. Several projects in raising awareness, such as regarding physical impairment, have been carried out with the staff for the purpose of breaking down paradigms and facilitating inclusion. In addition to this, Volvo started to offer industrial training courses for disabled people, in partnership with the National Service of Industrial Training (Senai). This way, the company develops professionals to meet not only its own needs but also those of the labor market.

The Volvo Traffic Safety Program, established in 1987, mobilizes governments, traffic agencies, companies, class entities, means of communication, schools, universities, and society in general for a safer and more humane traffic. It promotes seminars, debates, professional driver development programs, theater festivals, education for traffic in secondary schools, launching of books, and a number of other actions. Every year, the Volvo Traffic Safety Award is given to the best initiatives, by people or companies, in the promotion of better traffic.

The actions described here are just a small sample of what Volvo does in addition to developing transport solutions. There are countless social and cultural programs either established or supported by us. Many of these are sponsored via Rouanet Act, a cultural incentive law, or other pertinent legislation. Our company is among those that most contribute to culture in this country. We are aware of what each audience expects from us and, with responsibility, we endeavor to meet their expectations. What motivates us to do always more are the results achieved. And these are measured, above all, through the testimony given by the people who effectively participate in the programs and activities.

Our sense of social responsibility and the strong commitment to a more sustainable world are not just on paper. They make it out to the streets and cities. They help transform lives and form citizens. They make of the world around us a better place to live.

I usually say that I am the outcome of the awareness for a better world. I am one of the hundreds of children to which the SOS entity gave a chance for a better life. Through the Guarda-Mirim (Junior Guard) program, I received training and guidance for the professional world. But, above all, I received an education based on principles and discipline. Every morning, before going to work, we had to put on our uniform and march obediently under the attentive eyes of the Major – who let nothing get away. The sense of discipline that I developed at that time, at 13 years of age, has been of great value to me. Without it, I might have never made it so far in my personal and professional activities.

Today, when I am asked to help decide which programs will be launched for the disadvantaged community, I cannot help remembering that I have already been on the other side. I have felt on my own skin the joy of receiving secondhand clothing to replace the torn ones I was wearing and the relief of being able to wear shoes whose soles had no holes.

These memories only reinforce my belief in programs of this nature. For people who are assisted, they make all the difference. For those who implement them, they do too. After all, who is happier: the giver or the taker? Perhaps the only difference is that receiving is good for the body, while giving is good for the soul.

As I believe that work helps to shape character, develops determination, and forms individuals for life, I tried to do with my son what my father did to me. I gave him a shoeshine box when he turned 7 years old. I explained to him that, instead of getting an allowance, he should earn his own money by shining shoes for the whole family: father, mother, uncles, and grandparents. Not very thrilled, he did this for some time. But, at the first opportunity, he outsourced it to his younger brother who had shown interest in the novelty.

I then realized that the strategy hadn't worked because my son's reality is totally different from my own when I was a child. He doesn't have the same need to help supporting his family that I did. His world is a different one. So are his interests. And the challenges that he will face in life will certainly come from other sides. When I told him that he could perform tasks on the computer instead, his eyes shone with excitement.

In my way of seeing, need is still a major leverage for life. It makes people go into battle and look for different paths and alternatives. That's why social programs should never give anything for free, but rather establish the conditions for people to be able to earn their own livelihood. It's necessary to provide the tools that will stimulate the development of the potential in individuals, always in line with their interest, skills, and natural talents.

Volvo knows that the future of the planet will be the outcome of what we are doing today and that the organizations and their leaders play a fundamental role in this context. Therefore, it is necessary to have a sustainable management that addresses all the audiences and is included in a broader strategic plan. Everyone must do their share, here and now. We cannot simply blame the government, the politicians, the other companies and cross our arms.

Instead of focusing on the ones who are not doing their share, it is more productive to look at those who are – and be inspired by them. Then, it is important to start inside your own company, sowing the seeds in your own yard. After all, no one can change the world if they do not change themselves first.

14

Ethics no matter what

For Volvo do Brasil, ethics in business is mandatory. We never waive it, no matter what it may cost. If other people act differently, this is no excuse for us to change our behavior. We are a good, reputable company. And we want everyone who relates to us to feel this. If by any chance they don't, they should tell us. This is our permanent challenge to people who are around us and who follow our trajectory.

The audiences we relate to, better than anyone else, are capable of evaluating if we are being truly ethical in all our actions – and if our beautiful discourse really happens in practice. In order to hear what they have to say, we have created a number of tools and communication channels.

As usual, we begin in-house. Our employees can address suggestions, complaints, or denouncements with respect to ethics and conduct deviations directly to our Ethics Committee, by filling in a paper form available in a free access place or by using an electronic form. Moreover, they can talk to the Factory Committee, to the internal auditor, to their immediate superior, or directly to HR. Another way of stating their opinion is through the organizational climate survey held annually. It is also possible to get in contact with the head office in Sweden, using other available tools.

The external audience can state its opinion through Volvo do Brasil's website or through a hotline. Furthermore, customers and dealers can give their opinion through the satisfaction surveys that we carry out periodically. Alternatively, they can speak directly to the departments they have contact with.

Every feedback received, regardless of the way it comes in, is duly analyzed and referred to the competent area for the fitting actions. If the issuers identify themselves, they will get a reply on the topic.

In order to ensure that our employees act correctly and are not influenced by private, family members', or friends' issues that can lead them to promote favors or work against the interests of Volvo, we request everyone to fill in a Declaration of Conflict of Interests every year. In this document, they should report any and all possible conflicts that may influence their professional activity in any of the Volvo Group companies. All statements are analyzed, and the employees receive by e-mail the opinion regarding the conflicts declared, as well as the applicable guidelines.

In addition to the *Volvo Way* booklet and the global Code of Conduct, we also have a local Manual of Conduct that establishes clear guidelines for relationships with all audiences. The ethical principles are continually reinforced in the organization through the internal communication channels, e-learning, lectures by local and international specialists, and specific events.

We once gathered all leaders in an auditorium to discuss ethical issues of the company's everyday activities. By means of an electronic system, they were asked to vote for the most suitable answer in each situation from the point of view of ethics. This was a very interesting exercise, because it raised polemic issues that had not been openly discussed with the whole group yet. At the same time, it enabled us to clarify doubts and, in common agreement, establish parameters for actions.

The topic of ethics requires ongoing reflection. Behaviors that were acceptable in the past no longer are today. For instance, accepting a gift from a business partner was tolerable some time ago. Nowadays if the value of the gift is above the amount established by our internal policy, it must be returned. If that is not possible for logistic or cultural issues, it must be donated to charity. But, fortunately, few are the ones who still send us this type of gift. The audiences to which we relate are also much more aware of these matters, and many have adopted similar policies.

On the other hand, we also send gifts and invitations to events to our business partners, as part of our marketing actions. They all comply with our internal policy, though. As a general rule, they must be connected to the business, never characterize pure entertainment and, much less, be conditioned to closing deals or facilitating business. And, ultimately, it is up to our partners to accept them or not, according to their own code of conduct.

Just to illustrate the extent of our concern about ethics, we put on a play on this topic once. With humor and irreverence – without, however, missing the opportunity to provoke reflections – the play "To be or not to be: a matter of ethics" approached simple issues of everyday life. I remember one of the scenes which caused a visible reaction in the audience: a father, on berating his daughter for having taken a classmate's pen in school, said something like this:

– You shouldn't have done that, daughter. I am very disappointed in you.

Downcast and visibly embarrassed, she answered:

– I'm sorry, dad. I won't do it again.

And he continued in an angry tone:

– Why didn't you tell me you needed a pen? I would've brought you one from the company where I work.

The play was put on by a local theater troupe. It had the participation of professional actors and of Volvo employees, who attended theater classes for several months in order to be able to perform. In addition to several performances open to the public, a special edition was staged for the 2,000 employees of that time. A considerable logistic operation was needed to get everyone to the theater. On that day, there was also a loss in production, but that was no hindrance. After all, the topic on the agenda was of the highest relevance.

When you talk about ethics inside companies, people usually think about greater issues involving the top management and forget about the small day-to-day attitudes. But the principle is the same. The only thing that varies is the severity of the situation and the possible consequences. At Volvo, any and all conduct deviations are liable to penalties, regardless of the employee's hierarchical level. They are carefully analyzed by the Ethics Committee, made up of representatives from several areas and of the Factory Committee coordinator, with due care not to do an injustice.

On a given occasion, a representative from the Volvo Group's top management told me in a clear and emphatic way that, given my area of responsibility at Volvo do Brasil, I was one of the main guardians of the company's policies, moral, and ethics. Therefore, I should never allow anything that went against the corporate values to happen, anything that the Group's top executive would be unable to talk about with transparency, honesty, and without any embarrassment in front of television cameras – even if this meant losing business or shutting down the operation in the country.

This gave me even more strength to carry on acting in an ethical and sustainable way – and carte blanche to request the same posture from people in their day-to-day activities. The right to require that, however, implies a major responsibility: I have to be the first in setting the example. This way, I often end up being more demanding with myself and with the people who work directly with me than I would be with the others. My self-critical button is permanently on and always alert.

I consider myself blessed for working at a company whose values are so closely aligned with my own. Thus, I've never had to go against my principles or to make any concessions. I know that acting ethically is vital to establish solid and long-lasting relationships with gains for all parties involved, to establish bonds of trust with all audiences, and to be able to educate one's children properly. Above all, it is essential to have peace of mind.

Volvo do Brasil, for over three decades, has acted with much seriousness and honesty in the business world. It has kept its word and honored its commitments. It doesn't matter if we made less money because of this. Here, ethics makes itself present at all costs.

15

Consistent communication

Solid relations are built with trust and transparency, with open dialogue, and with consistent communication. We have always thought and acted like that. The commitment to truth has been the basis of our relationships. We thus gained credibility and started to count on the respect from all audiences we relate to.

Our employees are the first ones to feel the consistency and transparency in our way of communicating. As a practice, we always pass all the information on to them, even the most strategic like business plans and ambitions. Likewise, product launches are first shown to the internal audience. The news released to the external audience is also previously disclosed to the staff. That makes them really feel part of the company and clearly perceive the level of trust we place in them.

Different tools are used for internal communication. One of these is the *Viking* magazine, which has accompanied the company since it was established and is the flagship of a family of corporate communication products. With several sections, the magazine approaches the main events and activities underway in the different areas, as well as curious facts of everyday life, staff hobbies, and common behaviors. One of the most popular sections is the "Ghost Reporter" that, in a subtle and good-humored way, depicts employees' behaviors, giving tips and even raps over the knuckles for inadequate attitudes. This publication, which is one of the country's oldest in-house magazines, has already received several awards.

The "Viking" family also has other important members. The "Viking Online", available on the intranet, brings the main news of the week in addition to spot information. This same informative, in a printed format, is placed on more than forty bulletin boards spread throughout the company facilities. With daily update, these bulletin boards disclose information about the company, the market, and the openings available internally.

When official company information needs to be disclosed quickly to all employees, we print a "Viking Special", which can be easily handed out at the restaurants' exit and at the gates – at the beginning or end of each shift. If the topic is health, quality of life, or the Viking Association activity schedule, the channel is the "Viking Family", which is sent to the employees' home. The "Viking Reporter", on the other hand, shows programs, projects, and a retrospective of the best moments of the year on video.

Several magazines published in Sweden, electronically and in paper, bring us news of what is going on in the Volvo world and in the different business areas. Translated into several languages, they are distributed to all employees of the Group.

Our intranet is another extremely important and effective communication tool. It follows a global standard, used in all units of the Group around the world. Countless corporate information, as well as news from local and global business areas, is posted daily. Among the most often read are the organizational bulletins, which inform the changes in structure and the new appointments to different roles. All openings in Volvo do Brasil and in the Volvo Group are also widely disclosed.

There are different technologies available for contact and virtual meetings between staff members of all units around the world. This speeds up a great deal the information exchange and the decision-making process. The official language for communication is English.

The president of Volvo do Brasil has a communication channel permanently open to all staff. In his blog, he shares his visions and opinions on topics that affect the business – through video interviews or texts. At the same time, he opens space for questions or comments.

Virtual communication, however, does not exclude face-to-face communication at all. When there is something important to be personally informed by the president or the local board, we gather all employees at the Viking Association sports gymnasium.

In our day-to-day activities, there is a major concern to make all information reach the shop floor. This is hugely facilitated by the fact that we have self-managed teams. Under this management model, employees are split into groups, according to their work process. All members share the responsibilities and work with a minimum of direct supervision. Every week, each team representative holds a thirty-minute meeting to pass on to the group general information about the company, to provide relevant instructions for the execution of activities, and to discuss any other team related issues. On the day before, the representatives from each team have a previous meeting with their coordinators, to make sure that the information is passed on homogeneously.

Our Factory Committee, the first to be established in the state of Paraná, is also an important communication channel, as it creates a bridge between the staff and the company. With an office located in the middle of the plant, the committee has direct contact with workers from all areas and listens carefully to their suggestions and claims, which are later discussed with HR.

The Communication Meetings, attended by all leaders in the organization, are very popular. Following an annual calendar published at the beginning of each year, these meetings have become an important forum for the board to pass on information about the company and the business, for different areas to present their projects, and for special guests from outside the organization to lecture on topics of interest. Above all, these meetings are an open space for leaders to freely manifest their opinions, ask questions directly to the organization's main executives, make suggestions, and clarify their doubts.

The material presented is later placed in a virtual space shared by the leaders, so that they can pass on the information to their teams at the work meetings. In addition to the regular Communication Meetings, extraordinary meetings can be called at any moment to pass on spot information of an urgent nature. We often provide our leaders with a summary of the main points to be transmitted to their employees, to make sure that the information is cascaded down in a uniform way.

We believe that internal communication is of the utmost importance. If we want our employees to commit to the company like true partners, we have to share with them in a transparent and honest way our dreams, ambitions, accomplishments, and failures – the good and the bad news. By knowing exactly what is happening in the organization, people feel safer and more motivated to collaborate.

Our only concern is not to exaggerate in the dose. Information has to be passed on in the right measure, at the right time, and using the most appropriate channel for each situation. To do this properly, we must know our staff and the communication style that will be more effective for them. From there, we can formulate the strategic plans that will define clearly the messages to be passed on and the means to be used.

Even though we have many virtual tools at our disposal, we feel that the face-to-face communication is still the best. It enables us to perceive the impact of the information immediately, to listen to people's comments, and to clarify their doubts. In this sense, we offer a number of courses and training programs for our leaders so that they can communicate in an increasingly more effective way with their employees and with external audiences. For us, communication is much more than just passing on information.

Since a very early age, I realized that if I wanted to build a successful career in the corporate world, I would have to know how to communicate adequately. At the same time, I realized I lacked this skill. Given the simple environment in which I spent my childhood and the low level of formal education received during that period, this was definitely not a strong point of mine. I used to made mistakes when speaking and was hugely afraid of any audience. When answering the phone, I used to say:

– "Personner" department, good morning.

But the dream of one day becoming a leader made me struggle to make up for lost time. A lot of will power was needed to change things that were deeply inbuilt. And today I can say that I can communicate with any audience, without any embarrassment.

I have learned that good communication doesn't consist in just pronouncing the words correctly, in building sentences according to the grammar rules, and in having mastery of several languages. The content of your speech is what matters the most. You really have to believe in what you are saying and speak with enthusiasm, simplicity, truth, and good humor. You have to look people in the eye and speak from the heart. The greatest learning that I had, however, is that for communication to effectively occur, knowing how to speak is not enough. One must also know how to listen.

At Volvo do Brasil, the care we take with the internal communication is extended to the external one. We are often considered low profile, because we avoid overexposure on the media. We are restrained and consistent. We only speak when we really have something important to say or when we are asked to. If people come to us, we are always willing to listen and answer.

We are present in all the media we deem important for the business. Besides, our products and actions end up speaking for us and generating a high level of spontaneous media. We maintain a solid, professional, and very cordial relationship with the press. We respect their work and they respect our way of being.

There are countless external audiences to which we relate: governments, public and private institutions, companies, class entities, and several others. We adopt with all of them a very professional posture, avoiding excessive contacts. We do not waste our time nor theirs saying irrelevant things. We always bear in mind that messages must have clear content, consistency, and coherence. This way, we have built a high level of credibility over the years. And we have managed to keep a communication channel always open to all those around us.

PART III

WORLD-CLASS PEOPLE

16

The great secret

Many people ask me: "What is the secret of Volvo do Brasil's success?" With attentive eyes and all ears, they wait for the magic recipe which they imagine to contain highly sophisticated and complex ingredients – sheer mistake. The answer is very simple and can be said in a single word. But, in order not to be so direct, I begin by explaining the following.

For companies to achieve exceptional results, it is just not enough to have modern facilities, sophisticated equipment, adequate processes, well-defined organizational structures, and leading-edge strategic plans. Obviously, all these factors are important and necessary. But there is one element missing in this equation which is fundamental for the success of any organization. Then, finally, I say the magic word:

— People.

And I continue explaining: business plans, regardless of how elaborate they are, will never leave the drawers by themselves. They depend on people to gain life. The strength of an organization, therefore, comes from its people. Without them, the company is nothing more than a lifeless legal entity. Only committed, motivated, and engaged people are capable of transforming plans and dreams into reality.

After hearing that it is the people that make the difference, they act like they already knew or suspected that and move on to the second question: "How do you manage to have such motivated and committed employees? What is the great secret?" Again, attentive ears ready to hear, this time, something totally unprecedented. And, once again, what they hear is something very simple:

– The great secret is to treat people like people.

To this end, there is no need for any special tool or highly sophisticated equipment. You just have to adopt the basic and universal principles of respect and consideration as the foundation for the relationship with the employees.

When people feel respected, valued, and properly recognized, they give their best. Many times they surprise us, going beyond what they themselves felt capable of achieving. They move on from ordinary accomplishments to extraordinary ones.

We believe that people make all the difference. This belief, which we have held since the establishment of the company, is an outcome of the heritage that we received from the Volvo Group. It permeates our policies, practices, and day-to-day attitudes. We have always tried to understand our staff's desires and expectations, so that we could create a highly inspiring and motivating environment for them. That's how we learned it from the Swedes. And that's also the way we started to treat everyone, internally and externally.

At the beginning, as I have already mentioned, the confidence we had in our employees was misinterpreted by some, and this ended up generating unpleasant situations. We were serene and mature enough, though, to make the necessary adjustments. We did not allow that to impact on our belief in people, in their calling for the good, and in their potential for accomplishment.

But what does "treat people like people" mean in practice? The answer may be in a small plaque that I have on my table: "Treat other people as you would like to be treated yourself". This means treating the cleaning lady with the same level of politeness accorded to a visitor, only with less formality maybe; waiting for your turn in line, respecting those who have been waiting longer, even if they hold a position that is hierarchically lower than yours; being kind to everyone and not just to those who may benefit you in the future somehow.

For leaders, "treat people like people" means talking to their subordinates in the same way that they talk to their superiors. That is, with the same respect and consideration – and also with the same tone of voice. Those who raise their voice to their subordinates and speak softly to their boss either have a double personality or have no personality at all.

"Treat people like people" means beginning a feedback session by mentioning the strong points, the qualities, and the things that have been well done. This will minimize the effect of any negative things that are said after that. People are much more motivated by praise and by true recognition than by criticism – mainly when this is stated in a harsh and unthinking way.

"Treat people like people" means not firing someone for low performance, under normal conditions, without having provided that person with consistent feedback over time, indicating the points to be improved or corrected in an honest and transparent way. Everyone deserves at least one chance to try to improve their performance and is entitled to knowing what their real situation is.

"Treat people like people" means keeping in mind that people have feelings and will take them along wherever they go. The simple fact of stepping on the company's floor does not erase automatically from their memory all the problems and concerns that they might be experiencing in their personal lives. At some point, people will need support, understanding, or just a friendly word.

"Treat people like people" means being aware that people will invariably need to handle personal matters. Offering them the possibility to balance work with personal life is to respect their needs and to give them a chance to have a better quality of life. More than that, it is to encourage them to have other interests besides work and to develop skills that will broaden their worldview.

"Treat people like people" means having fair policies for compensation and benefits, which value people and recognize their importance as professionals. It means offering opportunities for training and development not only for work but also for life, forming not only professionals but also citizens.

"Treat people like people" means understanding that people are entitled to know the truth. Therefore, all information coming from the top of the organization must reflect reality and not a world of fantasy. Messages must make sense and be stated in an honest and transparent way.

"Treat people like people" means having empathy, displaying genuine interest for people, valuing individual differences, stimulating the development of the potentialities, recognizing a work well done and stating it with all the words. In short, "treat people like people" means, in the first place, *being* people.

At Volvo do Brasil, the same care and attention that we accord to the development of our products and services, we also have with our employees and with the work environment. We treat people like people. This is part of our culture and is what really makes of our company a special place to work.

We know that it is the energy of people that makes the complex organizational machine turn. Nothing can replace their commitment, dedication, and desire to make things happen. Like a master key, people can open any and all doors to success. For that, they only need to be treated like people.

OCEANO ATLÂNTICO
BAHAMAS
REP DOMINICANA
DOMINICA
SANTA LÚCIA
AÇORES
MARROCOS
ARGÉLIA
CABO VERDE
SENEGAL
GÂMBIA
GUINÉ BISSAU
NIGER
EQUADOR
BRASIL
AMÉRICA
DO
SUL
DIREÇÃO DE ROTAÇÃO DA TERRA
OCEANO
ATLÂNTICO

PART

IV

WORLD-CLASS ENVIRONMENT

17

Strategic HR

We have achieved the status of world-class company because we have world-class employees. We count on talented, enthusiastic, and deeply engaged people, who are always willing to go a step further, to go beyond their limits, to give their best. They deliver results for the company and for themselves. They have become our major competitive asset over the years, placing us in a standout position in the corporate world.

Like a powerful magnet, our way of being, our form of acting, the way we treat our staff, and the development opportunities we offer have attracted good and competent people. They identify themselves with our work philosophy and want to become part of our team.

In order to preserve this privileged situation, we are continually challenging ourselves. We want to be increasingly more a world-class HR: strategic, deeply involved in the business and in the management of the company, with credibility, and with the effective capability to add value.

We want to provide solutions that meet the desires of the employees and, at the same time, the interests of the organization and of the other audiences – with a long-term view that can help Volvo do Brasil to further increase its competitiveness.

The company has always given us support to take on that role. We have never lacked for space, freedom, and autonomy. In fact, these have only increased over the years. So did valuing and recognition, attested by our growing participation in the business and in the strategic decisions. On the other hand, leaders at every level of the organization have also displayed competence in people management, and this facilitates the HR actions a great deal.

I usually say that if HR doesn't do more at Volvo do Brasil, it's because of its own incompetence and not for lacking support from the company. I have never felt like the ugly duckling of the board. I have always had voice and opinion – not only when the issue is directly related to my area of responsibility but also when dealing with the company's business as a whole. I am part of the main decision forums, locally and in other Volvo units in South America. For over a decade, I have performed the role of deputy of the corporate president in his absence, which is not very common in the corporate world. This role is hardly performed by someone from HR.

Exactly like my colleagues of profession in this country, I have always defended that HR should have a seat in the main decision-making forums. However, not with the purpose of being in power and feeling valued, but rather to understand that the world does not revolve only around HR. There are other areas and issues in the company as important, or more, that need to be taken into account. Only when HR is involved in the business and in the higher issues of the organization, it will be able to establish policies and practices that effectively meet the needs of all audiences. And then it will, in fact, fulfill its role.

The world does not revolve around the company either. Going out there and discovering what other organizations are doing in HR can favor the appearance of important ideas and of revealing insights. In this sense, benchmarking is an interesting resource. The danger is when one simply "copies and pastes" what other people are doing. Just following the crowd, for fear of appearing outdated and out of tune with the world, can have disastrous consequences, which sometimes will be difficult to correct in the short term.

Policies must always be aligned with the company's development stage. One must have competency in adapting the trends to the needs of the company, instead of simply adopting all the different fashions that appear in the area. Some of these will disappear as quickly as they have appeared – and will not even be missed.

Many times, the strategic HR so much desired does not materialize. A more careful observation reveals shortcomings in both sides. At times, it is the HR professionals that lack good preparation, a suitable posture, and a strategic vision to be able to effectively contribute to the business. Other times, it is the organization that does not give them the opportunity to take on a more active role. The reasons can be widely different: consider that the guys from HR are filled with ideas and theories that are totally disconnected from the reality of the business, feel that their participation will not add much, or having had negative experiences in the past. Some company presidents even say that they have a strategic HR, but only not to sound outdated.

We must recognize, however, that there has been major evolution on both sides in recent years. Companies began to realize more and more that having a strong and active HR drives results for the business. Professionals, on the other hand, are investing more in their qualification, competency development, and preparation. The number of people interested in working in the area has also increased – by choice and not for lack of option.

Since the market is continually trying to create metrics and indicators to evaluate and justify the results of the area, I am often asked how to measure HR's level of contribution or even know whether it is effectively being strategic or not. For me, you just have to look at the results accomplished by the company. HR's performance must be reflected and embedded in them. But if you would like to use other indicators, you can measure the competencies development, the staff and the leadership performance, the organizational climate, and the level of pride and engagement displayed by the employees. HR has direct influence on all these items.

Another interesting test is to list the main corporate decision forums and check if HR is part of them – not just by being present, but effectively contributing to the strategic decisions and adding value. The fact of being at the top of the organization chart, by itself, does not mean that the area is strategic and valued. Much more than that is necessary.

HR actually has no other way out: it must be strategic and be present in the business. As far as that goes, there are no doubts. But, at the same time, it must never leave aside its essence. It must never forget that its higher mission is to take care of the human resources – that is, of all the issues related to the human side of the organization.

In order to do this properly, the area must have a solid and well prepared structure that can meet the needs of the company. Given the complex set-up of Volvo do Brasil as a joint company or "corporate condominium", we are structured according to the 1HR concept – that is, we have one single HR for the entire company. This way, we manage to optimize resources, obtain gains of scale, and promote synergy, in addition to unifying practices and procedures for all business areas and units. Likewise, we always try to align the global needs with the local ones.

Our HR structure comprises three basic functions: Center of Expertise, Service Center, and Business Partners. They are all interconnected and feed one another. At the same time, they work with the vision of the organization as a whole, without losing sight of the specifics of each business.

The Center of Expertise is responsible for the development of HR strategies, processes, and policies. The Service Center implements and manages HR services. The Business Partners give support to leaders in people management, according to the business strategies, policies, procedures, and current legislation.

In order to define the local HR objectives, we use as a starting point the strategic objectives of the Volvo Group, which serve as reference for all business areas, the specific HR objectives that are defined globally, and the guidelines of the *Volvo Way* and of the Code of Conduct.

Based on them, and on the principle that the human being is the main reference in our organization, we formulate our specific objectives that are later cascaded within the area, all the way down to the individual level. This way, all HR employees have a common north and realize how much their individual targets are important for the performance of the area as a whole. The area, in turn, contributes to the success of Volvo do Brasil's business, which generates results for the Volvo Group. Everything is interconnected. And each one's contribution, no matter how small it might seem, is fundamental for the sustainability of the whole.

At Volvo do Brasil, HR endeavors to add value and provide support for internal customers in a consistent way. With an extremely lean structure, we are strongly committed to understand what is really happening in each area, in the company, and in the business world. To this end, we need to be present. We have to listen to people, read between the lines, know what the problems are from up close, and analyze the cause instead of addressing only the symptoms. Otherwise, we will just be an office HR that is totally disconnected from reality and from life as it really is.

We have to understand how the company makes money and how we can help with that. We need to manage tangible and intangible assets properly; focus on actions that can build a healthy environment which stimulates and unlocks the potential of people; act decisively in the main issues and strategic changes of the organization; look at the whole and perceive that all parts are linked; keep an open mind, anticipating the world of the future. In short, we have to be on the front seat, like an efficient and highly reliable copilot that performs an extremely important role – in people management and in business strategy.

18

Constancy of purposes

Firmness and consistency have always been part of our journey. We knew exactly where we wanted to be and what path we should follow. Fashions have never fooled us. The siren song has never distracted our attention.

We were persistent in Human Resources. We stuck to our plans and transformed them into actions. Based on the company's needs, we formulated consistent and long-lasting policies. And the employees were the first ones to recognize their value.

We learned from the mistakes and slipups of the past. We punished those who abused the privileges and alerted the unsuspecting ones. We made the necessary corrections and carried on. Experience showed us that the majority could not pay for the error of a minority. The correct behavior of this majority reinforced our belief in people and made us hold true to our policies – with the appropriate adjustments that the natural evolution of the business world requires.

When I leaf through the HR strategic material developed in the last two decades, I see that practically everything came out of the paper, gained life, and was duly incorporated in the organization's day-to-day activities. Even the mental model map used to determine our north and give us the direction.

I also realize that, in spite of all the evolution, things have not changed that much in HR. In truth, history has repeated itself. Most issues and aspirations have remained essentially the same. They only gained a new appearance and more sophisticated, contemporary wording.

Many policies have not undergone any radical amendments over the years, just small adjustments required by each moment of history. A few have even matured and improved with time, like good wine – and like the Volvo products, which never lose their quality, only adapt themselves to the evolution of times.

And the reasons for our constancy are very simple. First, for the employees to understand that the organization thinks and acts coherently and with stability. Second, because most company's and staff's needs have remained the same, despite all the changes that occurred in the world.

On the other hand, new issues have come up on the horizon, bringing a nobler purpose for the organizations. Topics like ethics, citizenship, social and environmental responsibility, and sustainability of the business and of the planet have started to take up a good part of the agenda time, requiring actions and reflection. Employees have started to look at the capital-labor relation with other eyes, coming up with demands that require more strategic and complex actions by the employers. HR has also begun to have a more strategic role and a deeper involvement in the business. In order to deal well with these issues, one must detach from the past and tune into the modern world, but without giving way to fashions. Managing to separate the wheat from the chaff is the main question, though.

According to many career guidance specialists, I wouldn't be a good example of professional in the modern world. While they encourage people to change roles, areas, and even companies, I have worked all my life in HR and practically in a single organization. And, to make things worse, I intend to continue working in the same area and in the same company until I retire.

For some people, this may sound as a typical case of someone who has settled back and doesn't want to leave his comfort zone. Others may think it is a severe case of obstinacy and perseverance. For me, this is called constancy of purposes and the privilege of doing what I really like in a company that I admire, that values me, and in which I was able to help build the work environment I have always desired for myself.

I have learned that in life you have to define first what you want and then try to provide the arguments to justify your point of view. So, I always say that I remember no center forward or goalkeeper who wanted to change positions just because their area of activity was literally small or because they had been performing the same role for several years – quite the opposite, in fact. They all keep their roles up to the end of their careers and, if possible, would keep it for the rest of their lives.

I have never heard either that an athlete, an actor, a doctor, a race pilot, or any other professional who really does what he likes, and is duly compensated for that, wanted to change areas just because he had been in this one for a long time. His talent and passion for the activity do not allow this to happen. Due proportions maintained, that's how I have always felt. I have never wanted to change. Stop doing what I like has never seemed like a good option to me.

I have seen résumés of candidates that display a long list of jobs in a relatively short time span. For some people, this can indicate that these professionals have ambitions and enjoy new challenges. For me, this can be a sign that these people have not found themselves yet. They are jumping from place to place without really identifying with any of the activities. They are incapable of establishing long-lasting bonds with companies or people. They can't commit themselves to anything.

Those who have a different opinion about that will certainly also provide arguments to justify their position. And there is nothing wrong about that, as long as these are not mere excuses. Many people say that they changed areas because they wanted to escape from monotony, when in reality they lost their jobs. Others remain in a given area, without liking it, just because they want to stay in their comfort zone and are afraid of taking risks.

But one thing is certain: there is no single recipe that fits for all. People are different. And each one must find their own way to professional satisfaction. Some people love eating gilo. Others don't.

In all these years of work in HR, one day has never been the same as the next. There have always been new issues to be dealt with, problems to be solved, lessons to be learned and shared. The physical environment has changed, the working tools have been modified, many people have come and gone.

And I stayed there, firm and constant in my purposes. But I didn't stand still. I had to reinvent myself continuously in order to face the new demands and scenarios that appeared. I developed new competencies and enhanced those I already had. I took on other corporate areas of the company. I followed the evolution of things around me step by step – not as a mere spectator, but as an active participant who influences and is influenced all the time. I learned that to have new challenges and broaden one's horizons, it is not necessary to change areas, companies, or countries. Sometimes a change of attitude is enough.

Constancy has always given me a clear north to follow and generated commitment to the challenges that I took on at work and in other dimensions of life. I have learned that I can continue the same and, at the same time, be different.

Likewise, the constancy of purposes that has always characterized HR at Volvo do Brasil has been preserved even with the changes in the presidency and in the company board. We have maintained our policies in place not because we are nice guys, but because we believe that they are a fair exchange for what we receive from our employees.

We carry on believing that it is possible to do business with a nobler purpose than simply making money. We have a firm conviction that we can make a profit and, at the same time, continue to be a human company that values its workforce. This is our vision and our permanent challenge.

19

Special tools

Parading in the crowded sports gymnasium, to the sound of a thrilling song and the enthusiastic applause of the spectators, really got my adrenaline going. My heart started to beat faster and full of emotion. While I was holding the flag of East Timor, the team I represented at the Oliviking, the Olympic Games of Volvo do Brasil employees, I had a small sample of what athletes who take part in the opening parade of the real Olympic Games must feel.

The number of teams parading on the court was large. They were all doing their best, because the opening parade already counted points for the competition that would extend over the next four months, covering several sports.

The company president, a colleague from the board, and a number of employees from different areas were next to me helping to hold the big flag – and looking like a disorganized team. Trying to look like disciplined athletes though, we were performing the choreography recommended. But the lack of harmony was such that we could not avoid bursting into laughter.

In the bleachers, a large number of family members cheered and rooted for the beautiful performances and, of course, laughed at the uncoordinated ones. My family gave our choreography a zero and pointed out other teams as probable winners.

The event continued throughout that Saturday evening, following the ritual of the true Olympics. A video with Bernardinho, a famous Brazilian Olympic champion volleyball coach, specially made for that occasion, brought to the athletes a bit more of the Olympic spirit and reminded everyone that the important thing is to compete and not necessarily to win. Your desire to prepare yourself has to be stronger than your desire to win.

At a given moment, the lights in the sports gymnasium were dimmed for the triumphal entrance of Lars Grael, a Brazilian Olympic medal winner for sailing boats, who was carrying the Olympic torch. With his other hand, he leaned on a crutch. While he walked to the pyre, the entire audience was paralyzed by emotion. Tears flowed freely. Attentively, everyone heard the moving message of a true Olympic hero who, even after having had a leg amputated because of a boat accident, continued participating in competitions. His strong presence and his example of overcoming adversity brought huge inspiration not only for the athletes on the court but also for the spectators.

The party ended with a very cheerful ball. The music and the dance helped people to pour out the countless emotions they had experienced that night. On the way home, and still under the impact of the most striking scenes, I caught myself thinking, "This is Volvo do Brasil: moved by strong emotions." Our team, as my children had already foreseen, did not win the opening parade. But after four months of competition, we won the Oliviking.

Organizing these Olympic Games every three years may seem like something simple, but it is not. It requires a lot of work and mobilizes a huge number of people. In addition to the Viking Association, which organizes competitions in sixteen different sports and promotes a large treasure hunt to collect donations for charity institutions, the employees also participate actively organizing themselves into teams named after countries.

The number of participants has only increased over the years. In 2011, over 1,000 athletes, including beginners and veterans, participated in the fourth edition of the Oliviking. They did their best to overcome their own limits and to lead their teams to victory. During the months of competition, much adrenaline was released and strong emotions were displayed. Athletes and spectators joined together in a cheerful and fun partnership.

The Oliviking is part of Volvo's quality of life program and is just one of over eighty activities organized by the Viking Association. The big theme parties, held throughout the year, get together thousands of employees and family members in a single weekend.

The over 70,000 square meters of built area in the Viking Association, with facilities for different activities, are widely used. The company holds there several events, trainings, work meetings, and product launches.

After the work shift and on weekends, the staff and their family members fill up the fitness center, the soccer fields, the tennis courts, the racetrack, the hiking trails, the barbecue pits, the bar, and the party rooms where many weddings, christenings, and birthday parties have already been celebrated. During the week, many employees use the fitness center in alternative times, thanks to our flexible working hours practice. Those who work in the second shift use the soccer fields and other facilities even in the middle of the night.

During the hours when the facilities are not being used, it is time for the community of the surrounding areas to participate in a large number of activities linked to social projects: *capoeira*, soccer school, athlete of the future, dance, theater etc. During school holidays, the employees' children take part in the popular vacation camp.

About 10,000 people circulate in the Association every month. All sports, social, and cultural activities are aligned with our corporate values and with the standards set by Volvo's quality of life program. They count on the support from the company medical area and from other specialized professionals whenever needed.

I followed up closely everything that was built, because HR is the manager of the Association. I made sure that it did not become Fantasy Island, as it had happened to Volvo do Brasil in the beginning. There, as well, we had to make some adjustments in order to inhibit abuses. But we were successful. Like the Araucaria trees that surround it, the Association grew steadily in the more than thirty years that followed its establishment. Today, its roots are deep and strong. With the infrastructure of a true club, it gives us a competitive advantage in the business world.

I have described the spirit of the Oliviking and the work done by the Association just to give a flavor of the countless programs we have and of the strength they carry. With energy and joy, they mobilize thousands of people, promoting integration, development, quality of life, and citizenship. And this is just the beginning. There is much more.

Besides the Association, there are other spaces in the company for cultural events, activities of the Art in the Plant program, book fairs, exhibitions, and short performances that take place during working hours. Everyone likes to stop by the Cultural Space or by the Citizenship Street at lunch time whenever anything out of the ordinary is happening.

We also have a nice and hefty benefits package, whose differential lies not in the number of items granted, but in the way they are managed. In the health area, we offer numerous subsidies and services usually not offered by other health care plans, in addition to an excellent dental plan. Our main objective is to promote health through awareness raising, prevention, early diagnosis, and rehabilitation when needed. Instead of a "disease plan" that is only concerned in curing the problem after it has set in, we would rather have a "health plan". This is good for the employees and also for the company. The Volvo Dental and Medical Insurance Assistance (VOAM) is managed by Volvo itself.

Many bus lines are made available to facilitate employees' daily displacements. Meals include breakfast for blue-collars and partially subsidized lunch for all workers with a varied and balanced menu of options. The company also gives food coupons to those in the lower salary ranges. The life insurance we provide brings more tranquility to families in the event of an adverse occurrence.

The list of subsidies and benefits also covers other areas: study grants for secondary and college education, postgraduate studies, and language courses; flexible working hours, extended holidays through "bridge" days, extended maternity leave, home office after leaves, and day care center aid; bank branches and ATMs available in many places on the premises, cafeteria, coffee machines, travel agency for private travel, and library; special luncheons on commemorative dates or to celebrate results achieved; family visit programs that include a truck ride on the test track.

The Volvo Corporate Education Program offers employees a wide range of learning opportunities, from technical and behavioral training to literature and philosophy discussion groups. We work in partnership with several teaching institutions that design customized projects for us. One example is the Volvo MBA in Leadership and People Management developed in partnership with a local university and open to the community as well. Employees also have the opportunity to take part in international courses promoted by the Volvo Group in different places around the world.

Specifically targeted at our leaders, the Volvo Leadership Development Program offers courses based on five pillars: People Management, Business Management, Volvo Business Management, Quality of Life Management, and Worldview. Additionally, we provide executive coaching in order to address individual needs.

Volvo also adopts the competency-based management model as a basis for the employees' development regarding career, salary, training, and others. Roles are organized in blocks according to their nature: operational, technical, commercial, administrative, and managerial.

Every employee has their own Personal Business Plan, which is formulated with the help of a global electronic tool used throughout the Volvo Group. Based on the business area's or business unit's objectives, employee and leader sit together and set the targets to be achieved during the year. This is also an opportunity for both to discuss performance, development, and future prospects. In addition to this meeting held in the beginning of the year, two other ones are held: one at the end of the first half-year, for the purpose of assessing progress, and another at the end of the year, to measure the achievement of the objectives.

The opinion of the staff is very important. In order to measure their level of satisfaction in relation to different organizational aspects and their level of engagement, the Volvo Group conducts annually an organizational climate survey named Volvo Group Attitude Survey (VGAS). Translated into twenty-six languages, the survey is carried out in over fifty-five countries, electronically and anonymously. After the results are compiled, each area holds a workshop in which the employees and their leaders analyze together the results and formulate an action plan for improvements. Issues that depend on corporate actions are referred to the local board. Action plan monitoring is mandatory and duly recorded.

Volvo do Brasil shares its profit with the employees through a differentiated and very well structured plan, which is linked to the achievement of objectives. The Profit Sharing Plan (PLR) is divided into three blocks: corporate objectives and results of the company as a whole, objectives and results of each area, and objectives and results of each individual employee. Just to give you an idea of the amount paid out by the company, employees in the initial salary ranges received approximately ten salaries as profit sharing in 2011.

People with disabilities are very welcome in our company. In addition to adapting our facilities, we prepare our employees and leaders to receive them to make sure that inclusion really happens. One example of this is the number of people taking courses in LIBRA, the Brazilian sign language, to better communicate with their hearing-impaired colleagues. In the major events and gatherings we always provide simultaneous translation to the sign language.

It is important to be aware that many people who have some kind of disability end up developing other skills to a higher level than that of others. And this can become their competitive advantage. For instance, we have sight-impaired employees who very accurately perform tactile inspection of cab paint job quality, since their touch is more developed than that of people with regular sight.

The simple fact that they coexist with their difficulty and, even so, are active in the world already makes of people with disabilities examples of overcoming adversity. Those who are sound of body and mind and often complain of life can learn an important lesson with them: that the limitations and challenges presented by life can be overcome.

The concern we have for our employees has led us to prepare them even for the moment when they will leave the company. The With an Eye to the Future program was designed specifically to guide and prepare people for retirement or for a second career. Employees can join the program as from 55 years of age, with a view to retiring at the age of 60 at the latest. Despite having a pre-defined format that comprises psychological, financial, succession, health, and pension issues, the program is customized to address each person's specific needs and involves their family members. During the period in which employees are preparing themselves to leave the company, they also begin to work on their succession. The entire process takes place in full transparency, awareness, and with no surprises for neither of the parties.

Having a structured program to guide employees through their retirement planning process is extremely important. The moment to retire will invariably come around one day, regardless of whether people want to think about it or not. So, it is better to be prepared – and begin to realize that there is life outside the company.

Another benefit, which will make a lot of difference to people's pocket when they retire, is the monthly contributions deposited by the company for each employee in the Volvo pension fund, named Viking-prev. If employees want to increase the amount of money in their accounts, they can also make voluntary contributions. The administrative costs of the fund are fully covered by the company.

As can be seen, the list of benefits, programs, and activities undertaken by Volvo do Brasil is quite long – and there is still a lot more. These are all special tools widely used to foster a healthy environment, in which people feel motivated to work and realize that their value is recognized.

With higher quality of life and opportunities to experience things that deviate from the typical arid environment of a vehicle manufacturer, our employees broaden their worldview and develop. They become happier people and more responsible citizens. This increases their level of engagement with the company. Do I have to say more?

20

New old challenges

In order to remain in the leading edge of people management, I can only see one way: to maintain a strong HR that has consistent policies, is able to make the difference, and is permanently prepared to meet the demands of the world of today and of tomorrow.

As previously mentioned, HR must be strategic and involved in the business. But it cannot remain there all the time, given that its primary mission is to deal with issues related to the human side of the organization. Its major challenge, therefore, is to balance the attention given to business and to people management – that is, to meet the needs and desires of both sides. In other words, it has to keep an eye on the cat and the other on the fish.

When we talk about the future, what usually comes to people's mind is a world completely different from the one of today. In this imaginary world, the issues we would tackle in HR would be other ones – totally different and unprecedented.

In real life, however, things are not exactly like that. If we compare the HR from the past with the one of today, which at that time was the HR of the future, we will see that, regardless of how much we have evolved, of the new ways of thinking that have appeared, and of the different tools that have been developed, some topics remain the same. They may seem like new ones. But a more perceptive and experienced look will soon recognize the well-known old topic underneath a new guise or disguised in the middle of a modern and sophisticated diagram. In its essence, however, it remains the same.

One of the new old topics on the HR agenda is to attract, retain, and develop people. When I started to work, this was known as Recruitment & Selection and Training. The names have changed, but the needs remain the same. We must become an increasingly more attractive employer that manages to bring to its staff the best professionals. But bringing them is not enough. We must be able to keep them, preferably happy and fulfilled, so that they can give their best.

In order to do that, we must offer a compensation and benefits package that is competitive in relation to the market, a great work environment, a wide range of training and development opportunities, conditions that allow people to reconcile professional life and personal interests and so on. This great challenge, which has always been on the HR agenda, has become even tougher today given the shortage of qualified professionals in some areas and the fact that many companies have started to compete in equal conditions.

Another new old topic of the utmost importance is the development of leadership. More than ever, we must train and qualify our leaders to take on the role of coaches – another beautiful term that has recently become a buzzword. We also have to keep in mind that, when employees look at their leaders, they see the company in them. Therefore, leaders must in fact personify the organizational values and display them in their actions, attitudes, and decisions, not only inside the company but also before external audiences.

The transition of generations is another subject that is forever present. How to get young people filled with energy and technology, who nowadays answer to the name of generations Y, Z, alpha, and other letters that are still coming up, to take on roles that have been performed with high levels of competence and experience by the generation that is retiring, without any loss of knowledge? In the past, we did not have a string of letters, but we already worked to avoid a clash of generations and cultures.

Preserving the level of motivation and engagement of the staff is a permanent challenge. What makes people get up every morning and go to work willing and in a good mood? What makes them remain in a company for years in a row and continue delivering results with the same level of passion and quality? What type of work environment do they need to be able to leave a legacy? These and other questions are always hammering in the head of the HR guys.

And what about the Factory Committee then? It is impossible to keep it out of the company agenda, because it is present all the time – even when it is not expected to get involved in certain issues. Its importance is undeniable and many were the contributions it has made over the years. The current model, however, needs to be revised. We must retrieve the primary function of the Factory Committee, which is to represent all employees, adding value both to them and to the company, with a long-term view.

Union relations and collective negotiations have never left the agenda either. Much the opposite, they gain more space on it every year. I would say that this is the topic that concerns us most today, since it has become a major threat to the company's competitiveness and to the continuity of our management practices in HR.

We have here a good example of what a new old challenge is: the same topic, discussed with the same leaders of the metalworkers' union for nearly thirty years, gains different hues in every moment of history, given the new ingredients and interests that appear. The negotiations have never been easy. In the past, however, they had a rationale. Considerations were made and accepted. When necessary, both parties made concessions with a view to closing a win-win deal and, most of the times, everyone came away from the negotiation table satisfied with the results achieved.

Unfortunately, things have changed a lot in recent years. In truth, we haven't had negotiations in the true meaning of the word. We have simply been forced to accept what was being imposed on us. Otherwise, the consequences would be even worse for the company at that moment.

That has left us with a bitter taste in our mouths. The more we become a reference for the market, the more we are pressured by the union. In a way, we are more demanded for being among the best companies to work for in Brazil, for offering excellent benefits, and for having leading-edge policies. Aware of all this, they demand continually more from Volvo. They are not satisfied in closing with us on the same amounts that are closed with other manufacturers.

The situation we are experiencing nowadays reminds me of a balloon: the union leaders think they can always fill it up a little more. But they don't realize that if they blow it up too much, it will explode, and everyone will end up losing. Volvo Group's investments will be directed to other units in other countries. The company will lose competitiveness in the country and in other markets, which will have an impact in the number of jobs offered. This will affect the workers and the union directly. Our major challenge is to make everyone understand this, so that the situation can be reversed.

During all these years of relationship with the union, many interesting episodes took place and some will never be forgotten. One of them was the fact that I climbed on the truck that was being used as a platform, from where they were making inflamed speeches to the employees during an assembly, without having been invited.

I did that on impulse, when I realized that the assembly was being taken down the wrong path. Caught by surprise, they allowed me to speak. And from up there, with all the climate of tension and animosity that hung in the air, I managed to improvise a few words. The employees applauded. The union, of course, hissed. But the fact remains that this helped to solve the standoff that had been created, and an agreement could finally be closed and approved in the assembly.

Later, I was praised for my courage. But for me, it was more a desperate and unthinking act in an attempt to solve a situation that could have disastrous consequences. I wouldn't do it again, at least not in the same way. I did climb again on their truck, on another occasion, but it was on their invitation.

Perhaps, in a not very distant future, we will manage to see the company and the union openly placing their points of view for the employees in an assembly. This would be an innovative, much more mature, and rational way of undertaking this process, which has been extremely wearing for all. Then we would, in fact, have a win-win relation.

I was recently invited to the inauguration party of the Union Board of Directors. To my surprise, when I got there, I was invited to join the main panel, next to the union leaders and several local authorities. And more: I was given the microphone and asked to speak. I found myself in a very tricky situation. But later, I came to realize that it had been a gesture of maturity on their part and also a display of consideration towards me. After all, in spite of our diverging positions, we have managed to preserve an open and sincere relationship over the years. What was really difficult, though, was to hear them speak proudly of their victories over the companies, at the same time that they projected images of assemblies and strikes on the screen – and, even more difficult, was having to applaud.

After a few years of complicated and highly stressful negotiations, the latest rounds have been slightly more decent – if one can call them that. I hope this is an indication that things are really beginning to change, and that the light is finally beginning to appear at the end of the tunnel, pointing the way to the dialogue, transparency, and rationality that we desire so much. But only the future will tell.

The fact is that we will still have new old topics on the HR agenda for a long time. They are challenges of the present with the face of past. The main question is how to deal with them in a way that is more efficient and best suited to the new times.

When the context changes, new approaches, techniques, and tools are required. More than that, we need to take a fresh look at things so that we can see other angles and glimpse what has not been seen yet. Or maybe it is just necessary to do what has already been seen in the past, but that no one had the courage to put in practice. At any rate, we must see the new world with the new demands, but at the same time we have to treat the old demands in a new way. Otherwise, we will be likely to make the same errors of the past. And this is exactly what we do not want.

21

Leadership driven by the Volvo way

In addition to producing vehicles, we also "produce" leaders – leaders of excellent quality, of high performance, and suitable for export. They are the mirror of our organization and personify Volvo's values, principles, and culture.

Most of them are seen by the employees as role models and source of inspiration. They are self-confident and believe in what they do. They manage to see and go further. They transform objectives into accomplishments.

We need the commitment from all employees to achieve our purposes. But, above all, we rely on the strength of our leadership. Our management style requires leaders that search for excellence through people, that aim at extraordinary results, and that are capable of taking the company to increasingly higher levels.

The development of leaders is widely facilitated by the world-class environment that we have in our organization. The autonomy, the freedom to dare, and the access to new technologies, leading-edge ideas, and reference practices enable people to grow and develop. Many times we see the leadership capability emerge in individuals whose profile would not appear in books dealing with this topic.

I usually say that talent and competence are independent of gender, ethnic origin, or social class. Leaders are born and grow up in any area. And no boss is capable of stifling their appearance – at least, not for a very long time. Someone will always end up perceiving those people whose mindset is totally aligned with what is expected and desired in a leader. If they are not recognized by their own boss, they will be by other managers or even by other companies. It is just a matter of time.

The Volvo Group defined in the past the twelve competencies that were essential for its leadership. Recently, the Group adopted the Leadership Pipeline concept, based on the book *The Leadership Pipeline: How to Build the Leadership Powered Company* by Ram Charam, which is an enhancement of the concept that had been in use before that. The new methodology proposes different sets of competencies for different classes of leadership – Emerging Leader, Leading People, Leading Leaders, and Leading Business – establishing a relation between the skills, capabilities, attitudes and the different levels of complexity of each role. Competencies are subdivided into five areas: Strategic Thinking, Inspiring Leadership, Courage & Integrity, Execution, and Self-Management.

The identification of potential leaders in each area is done annually through a global practice called Talent Review. All bosses evaluate their direct reports and point out those they consider having leadership potential. They justify their nominations by informing the main results achieved, the strengths, the opportunities for development, and the future roles these professionals may take on. These nominations are later validated by the local board.

From then on, the nominees begin or intensify their development process, through the Volvo Leadership Development Program (PDLV). Thanks to partnerships established with a number of leading-edge institutions, the program offers the best options available on the market in terms of executive qualification. The Volvo Group also carries out international leadership development programs that are attended by professionals from all over the world.

Through these mechanisms, countless people have been appointed to take on leadership positions in new openings or through succession processes, both in Volvo do Brasil and in other units of the Group. The vast majority of the leaders who hold the highest positions in our company today were developed internally. Rarely have we had to look for someone on the market. We have always had excellent options in-house. And this makes our work a lot easier.

I don't play chess. But one of the things I practice most in the company is corporate chess. Placing the right person in the right position at the right time is an art form – and a major challenge. When the move is well done, all parties involved are pleased and satisfied.

Thanks to my knowledge of the organization, I have been able to contribute to the choice and movement of countless leaders. In order to do the right move, it is imperative to have a clear vision of the whole and try to glimpse the next two or three career movements for that person, bearing in mind the future openings that will come up in the organizational chessboard.

At Volvo do Brasil, where several business areas are located within the same industrial complex, our leaders are not limited to the boundaries of their areas. They are part of the organization's talent grid as a whole. This way, when we have an opening, the chances of finding someone in-house are multiplied threefold. Globally, people are sometimes surprised by some of our moves. In general, they only consider the talent grid of their own specific areas and forget that in Brazil we have a privileged condition that opens up countless possibilities for us. This is one more advantage of the "corporate condominium".

Looking at the organizational chessboard, with all the possibilities that come up, and at the talent grid, with all the options it offers, is an extremely interesting exercise. At the same time, it requires deep reflection and a high degree of responsibility in order not to interfere in people's life in the wrong way. Like a chess game, this is something that takes time. There are many things on the line that must be carefully appraised.

I have already spent many sleepless hours wondering what to say and what to recommend in some cases. I could clearly feel the weight of responsibility on my shoulders. Most of the times, I was pleased to see later that the sequence of movements brought very positive results for the business and for the people involved. This means that it was the right move. Sometimes, however, I came to the conclusion that the move wasn't so right. But that's OK. You can't win all the time. The important thing is to absorb learning and get ready for the next match.

As head of the HR area, people always ask me what the secret to becoming a respected and successful leader is. I answer that there isn't an off-the-shelf recipe that will be good for everyone. After all, people are different. And so are the organizations' culture and the business segments. That's why each one has to discover their own way of getting there, according to their reality.

Some requirements, however, are basic for people who would like to be good leaders in the corporate world: good academic background, knowledge of people management, languages, and emotional balance. But having all these is useless if the person does not have posture, character, and is not capable of relating to others. I have observed that attitudes are extremely important. While some of them help building a solid career, others are only effective in destroying it.

I have no intention of giving leadership lessons here, nor do I feel competent to do that. At any rate, I mention below some points that I deem important and that may help to shed light on this issue. They are the outcome of my observation and reflection in more than forty years of corporate life, during which I have already seen a bit of everything with respect to this topic – or nearly everything.

Attributes and attitudes that can drive a career

- Expressing yourself with clarity and objectivity. Knowing how to sell your ideas. Focusing on the right issues. Going straight to the point without beating around the bush.
- Being capable of transiting in any environment and adapting to the context. Displaying behaviors that fit the situation.
- Participating in projects that extrapolate your area of action, both in the company and outside it. In addition to stimulating development, these projects will function as a showcase to exhibit competencies and skills.
- Being result oriented. Being capable of delivering according to expectations and beyond them. Creativity is always highly valued.
- Enjoying challenges. Endeavoring to surpass yourself constantly. Going beyond tiredness.
- Having an authentic desire to make things happen. Looking for ways to get there. Never expecting things to fall into your lap.
- Being persistent and obstinate. Keeping yourself firm in your purpose, in spite of any difficulties that may appear. Being aware that there is always a price to be paid or something to be given up.
- Having moral power, regardless of having formal power. Having authority is not enough. People have to recognize it. And this is something that you have to gain. No one can give it to you.
- Having a moral and ethical conduct that serves as an example and reference for others.
- Being concerned with costs and, at the same time, with revenues. Considering the cyclic aspect of business. Having flexibility and agility in dealing with the ups and downs of the business segment.
- Detaching yourself from titles and other symbols of status. They can come as recognition – or not. They must never be the target per se.
- Increasing self-knowledge. In particular, getting to know your strengths and learning how to explore them.

- Having self-control. If you cannot manage yourself, you will not be able to lead other people.
- Treating people as you would like to be treated, regardless of the position they hold. "What's sauce for the goose is sauce for the gander," as the old saying goes.
- Having high self-esteem. You must like yourself first to be able to like other people.
- Learning from everyone and everything – including from your own mistakes and from the mistakes of others.
- Being capable of developing leaders in your team rather than just followers.
- Having healthy habits and attitudes that generate positive energy. Being in good terms with life. Developing spirituality.
- Practicing physical activities. In addition to increasing your energy, they will help you to relax and relieve tension from everyday life.
- Cultivating healthy relationships outside the work environment. Counting on support from family and friends is fundamental to overcome the ups and downs in your career.
- Having a life plan that addresses other dimensions in addition to career. Looking at life as a whole and being capable of focusing on the different priorities in every moment of existence.

Pitfalls to be avoided – they do not help to move up the corporate ladder and even make you lose points

- The blowfish effect: allowing yourself to be inflated by your new title or role. Being too much in love with yourself.
- Being arrogant and displaying an air of superiority towards other people. Considering yourself irreplaceable and omnipotent.
- Forgetting that the power that derives from your position is granted to you under a lending agreement. One day, it will have to be given

back, together with the company's microphone that enhances the power of your voice and with the corporate surname that opens doors in so many places.

- Paying too much attention to what you hear on the office grapevine, instead of trying to learn the official version of the facts.
- Being jealous of other successful professionals in the company. That's the worst thing possible. It only causes damage to people and careers.
- Moaning and groaning about things that have already happened and cannot be brought back. Having difficulty in turning the page and moving forward.
- Seeing ghosts where there aren't any. Thinking that people are always trying to pull the carpet out from under you. Being on the defensive all the time.
- Having too much information and too little focus. Taking countless courses and never being able to put that knowledge into practice. Floundering about in the basic issues of everyday life.
- Making a lot of noise and delivering little results. Talking more than what you can effectively do and deliver.
- Making mistaken promotions, giving power to people who are not capable of wielding it.
- Forgetting your role as a leader and representative of the company and joining in the chorus of complaints, instead of going in search of solutions.
- Resisting changes. Being unable to keep up with the natural evolution of things. Trying to remain in your comfort zone.

Some aspects of the corporate world that no one can explain

- Heaven and Hell have no boundaries. One day the person is in heaven and the next one is at rock bottom. The same people who praise you today may throw stones at you tomorrow.

- Some people can fall up. When everybody thinks the coffin is ready to be closed, the person comes back to life in another position – even better than the previous one. That's what I call having connections to the powers beyond.
- A lot of energy is still spent with egos and vanities. It could light up an entire city.
- Being is not enough. You have to look like it too. Otherwise, no one will believe you are.
- When you need help in any work or project, always ask someone who is already busy. Never ask someone who has time left. The latter will find an excuse, while the former will find a way of fulfilling your request.
- Treat all people nicely. One of them may become your boss tomorrow – and may have an excellent memory.
- Brazilians who take part in expatriation programs come back more Brazilian than ever.
- The most efficient plan is not always the one that was best formulated and that deployed the best resources. The best plan is always the one that works. The color of the cat doesn't matter as long as it catches the mice.
- Perfect is the enemy of good. Knowing when to stick only to good results is the key. Sometimes people waste huge amounts of time with details that are not so relevant and that will not influence the final result. There is nothing more useless than doing useless things with perfection.
- Many times it is not possible to treat everyone in the same way. In these cases, justice is done by the difference and not by the equality.
- It is easier for leaders to be expelled from the work environment because of behavioral aspects than because of lack of technical competence.
- Sometimes it is better to spend time in labor exile, waiting for the dust to settle down, than moving forward at any cost and failing. Expatriation can be a way out.

- Creating a bad image doesn't take very long. Erasing or changing it can take a whole life. And there will always be someone not willing to forget it.

All the points I have mentioned above stem from my perception rather than from any form of scientific work. Therefore, they bear no warranty seal. It is up to each one to evaluate them and come to their own conclusions. However, I can say that the greatest leaders I have met in life think along the same lines – to a greater or lesser extent.

Many people have asked me if individuals are born with the attributes of leadership or if these can be acquired over their lifetime. For me, it is much more a matter of dedication and sweat than actually genetics. Becoming a true leader sometimes takes a while. And there are no shortcuts. You must take each step of the journey consciously. You have to truly want it, believe that you can get there, and be willing to pay whatever it costs.

The effort is worth it, though. An organization that strives for success will always need good leaders, who are capable of deciphering the most complicated situations, of pointing out solutions and even building them if necessary. It will require leaders who are capable of mobilizing people towards a common objective, who inspire trust and have credibility, who act ethically and wisely, who feel that they are the company – and, above all, who have the company look and act the company way.

[illegible]

… know … and may have an excellent memory.

[illegible]

These cases must be treated by the difference and not by the equality.

- It is easier for leaders to be expelled from the work environment because of behavioral aspects than because of lack of technical competence.
- Sometimes it is better to spend time in labor exile, waiting for the dust to settle down, than moving forward at any cost and failing. Expatriation can be a way out.

22

Map of the stepping stones

On the little farm where I lived as a child, there was a stream. The trees with the tastiest fruits were on the other bank. This served as a motivation for us to cross the cold water and go to the other side. After doing this a few times with difficulty, I noticed that the people who were more experienced knew a path that had been created naturally by the stones. Following this path, the crossing was much faster and easier.

It was at this point that I discovered the importance of knowing the stepping stones. Having a map of them, even if only mentally, was fundamental to reaching the desired destination in safety and with higher speed.

Likewise, drawing a road map for an area or a company is essential to reach the fruits that are on the other bank – the gains and results. In order to begin drafting it, you must first understand what is happening on this side of the river. You have to study carefully the current situation to know exactly where you are stepping. Then, you can define the desired position to be reached in the future and the main objectives you intend to achieve.

Before trying to move out of the current situation and reach the desired position, it is necessary, however, to have total clarity on factors that may help or complicate the crossing. This evaluation can be undertaken in a number of different ways, and each one certainly has their own. But, if the objective is to do this in a more structured way, there are two tools that can be very helpful.

The first one, called SWOT analysis, helps to clearly map the strengths, weaknesses, opportunities, and threats. This can be done in relation to the area, to the company, and to the business environment as a whole which has countless variables.

The PESTEL analysis, on the other hand, can be used to survey the political, economic, social, technological, environmental, and legal factors that may impact on the decision-making process.

Another aspect worthwhile analyzing is the past. In addition to history, it can be a great reference, given that it shows clearly what worked well in the area or company and what didn't.

The next step is to define the actions and strategies that will be necessary to achieve the desired position. Therefore, it is time to draft the Strategic Plan. With a systemic view, that comprises the analysis of the environment as a whole and of the different interconnections, it will create a bridge between the current situation and the desired one.

The supporting pillars of this bridge are the culture, the values, the principles, and the code of conduct, which will enable you to reach the future with responsibility and sustainability. The corporate governance system will also serve as a support and must be respected. You must be aware that the most important actions and decisions will have to be previously anchored in order to have a higher chance of acceptance. A good strategy is to discuss them with all those who are involved in the decision-making process before formally referring them for approval.

You must also be aware that there will always be costs to achieve an objective – and not just financial ones. A lot of energy will have to be spent as well. Therefore, you have to evaluate the cost-benefit ratio carefully and define the price you are willing to pay to get there.

Another important point is analyzing the way in which the work is being done and the mindset that is being applied. If they are not proven efficient, perhaps it is the moment to innovate, to think differently, to make use of creativity, and to try other options.

In my view, these are the main issues that should be taken into account when you are drafting the road map for an area or a company. In order to facilitate understanding, I have listed below some basic questions that can help in this task:

- What objectives do you intend to achieve? Where do you want to be? When? (Desired position)
- What are the strengths, weaknesses, opportunities, and threats of the area, of the company, and of the business environment as a whole? (SWOT analysis)
- What political, economic, social, technological, environmental, and legal factors may have an impact? (PESTEL analysis)
- What worked well in the past? What didn't? (History and learning)
- What actions and strategies will be required to get there? (Strategic plan)
- What values and principles will support the journey? (Code of conduct)
- What investments will be necessary in terms of money and energy? What price are you willing to pay?
- Where can you innovate? What can be done in a more effective and creative way?

When I drafted a road map for the HR area for the first time, I began to have a clear vision of the whole. I realized the importance of the area within a broader context. I understood that strategies must be aligned with the business, that all parts must be in tune for the whole to work properly, and that the whole will always be greater than the sum of the parts. And, finally, I came to the conclusion that excellence will only be achieved through people.

This same mental model has also been of great value in drafting a road map for my life as a whole. In addition to career, my road map comprises other dimensions: family, finances, health, leisure, social life, spirituality etc. In order to address each of these properly, I always start from the point where I am and define where I want to be. Then, I evaluate my strengths and weaknesses with respect to the objective intended and establish the necessary actions to get there.

By doing this type of analysis, I realized some interesting things: I don't need many hours of sleep, which allows me to have more time available for other activities. The best way to replenish my energy is by doing physical exercises. And, while I am exercising, I mentally solve a number of issues that have arisen during the course of the day. Most of the times, these characteristics have been converted into advantage and have helped me to achieve my targets.

It is important to highlight, however, that each person has to discover their own competitive advantage, which can be applied in any context. What works for someone does not necessarily work for someone else. It is also worthwhile reminding that, even though all aspects of life are linked and depend on each other, in certain phases we will give more attention to some of those and not so much to the others. But that's OK. The important thing is not to lose sight of them and retake them as soon as possible.

The road map for our life is permanently under construction. As we mature and accomplish some of the things, our interests naturally change. What we wanted so badly to achieve in the past maybe no longer makes sense today. At the same time, other interests appear on the horizon. Likewise, the force of the waters in the river also changes the place of the stones. And to continue crossing in safety, the map of the stepping stones must be constantly updated.

MAP OF THE STEPPING STONES
ENVIRONMENT AND ITS IMPACTS
(PESTEL ANALYSIS)
PAST
HISTORY
REFERENCE
LEARNING
PRESENT
SCENARIOS
(SWOT ANALYSIS)
INTEGRATED
STRATEGIC
PLAN
FUTURE
DESIRED POSITION
AMBITIONS
OBJECTIVES
SUPPORTING
PILLARS
CULTURE
VALUES
PRINCIPLES
CODE OF
CONDUCT
GOVERNANCE
THE WHOLE IS GREATER
THAN THE SUM
OF THE PARTS

PART V

A LOOK TO THE FUTURE

23

Thank you, Swedes. Welcome, Americans

After a solid relationship of many years, we are in a way cutting the umbilical cord that links us to Sweden. Starting in 2012, almost all Volvo do Brasil's operations stopped reporting to Europe and began to report to the new area called Americas, which is headquartered in the United States.

In an emotional tone, Swedes and Brazilians thanked each other for the partnership of trust and professionalism, which remained unshaken through the good and bad moments of a successful journey of over three decades. This cycle closes exactly this year in which Volvo do Brasil celebrates its 35th anniversary.

The change in the reporting line stemmed from the restructuring of the Volvo Group, promoted by the new global CEO, which came in force in January of this year. Obviously, a change of this magnitude is not implemented overnight. It will take some more months for everything to fall into place.

In the new structure, the Volvo Group was organized into geographical areas: Americas, EMEA (Europe, Middle East, and Africa), and APAC (Asia and Pacific). Each area became responsible for all the Group's brands and businesses in its region.

In our case, the Trucks division, which until then had been responsible only for the Volvo trucks, became responsible for the other brands belonging to the Volvo Group: Renault Trucks, UD, Mack, and Eicher – for all Latin America except Mexico.

As soon as the new global organization was announced, speculations began to pop up in Brazil. Initially, they were about the definition of the local organization. Later on, about the Americans: "Will we get along with them after being used to the Swedish way for so many years? Will they change everything? Will they accept our way of doing things?" Direct, objective, and focused on results – this was the image of the Americans that came to our minds.

With so many question marks and without knowing exactly what to expect from our new bosses, we held a seminar on intercultural settings as soon as possible. At the opening, someone said that now we would really have to learn how to speak English, because the language that we used to communicate with the Swedes wouldn't be enough anymore. All jokes aside, the meeting made it clear that the Swedish and the American cultures are very different. And so are people's attitudes and behaviors, even though they are all part of the Volvo Group.

The debate led to reflection on the opportunities that the organizational structure change could generate, given the increase in our scope of responsibility. We clearly realized that we all had an urgent task to perform: to change our mindset. Instead of thinking only about the Volvo brand, we would have to work under the multi-brand concept. The Volvo blood that runs through our veins had gained a special color brought in by the other brands.

And the Americans, curious to learn about Volvo do Brasil, their new area of responsibility, did not delay visiting us. The Swedish flag, usually flown to receive our visitors, politely gave way to the American one.

The Americans did not come in dragging clogs like the Swedes had done thirty-five years before. But they came with the same humbleness and surprised us in the same way. What we most heard was: "If it ain't broke, don't fix it." They emphasized all the time that they wanted to learn with us so that, together, we could give continuity to the good work we had been doing with the Swedes up to then. This put us at ease and made us very optimistic. We hope that the initial enchantment will not fade and that the good impression we had will consolidate. We are experiencing one of those troubling moments of transition when nothing will be the way it used to be. At the same time, no one knows how it is going to be.

We are going to work hard for this new relation to become a successful partnership, hoping that it will give continuity to our trajectory of accomplishments and will result in gains for both sides. We have our own identity. We will continue doing what we know how to do. But we are always open and receptive to new cultures and ways of thinking.

We would like to deeply thank the Swedes for the vast learning they have afforded us over the course of all these years; for the consideration and respect with which they have always treated us; for having believed in our capacity even before we did; for having shown their support and loyalty in times of failures and of glories; for having established with us a professional and friendly relation, which filled us with energy and showed us that it was possible to achieve great results – and that gives us today the confidence to experience another culture and to start new relationships.

When I look at my life and at all that I have built, I am also deeply grateful. I have done nothing alone. I have always counted on the support and affection of the people around me – starting by my parents, who put me in this world, and by my siblings, who together with me experienced the difficulties and joys of growing up. Thanks to the lessons learned in the family, I was able to carry on with confidence and determination and to establish later on my own family, which is today my most precious asset.

In the work environment, I have also met a lot of people who helped me to write my story. I remember in particular the people who patiently taught a shy and hard-working office-boy the first lessons about the corporate world. And those, already in the big city, who believed in the potential of a young man, full of dreams, and gave him the chance of a job.

Many people gifted me with their teaching and friendship throughout my life. And maybe they don't even know how important they were to me. But, regardless of that, they have a very special place in my heart. Others are part of the present moment and serve as a role model and inspiration to me. And there are those that will still be placed in my path and who will teach me the lessons that I still need to learn. To all of them I am hugely grateful.

At Volvo do Brasil, we will continue to be in contact with Sweden, since we have many work processes in common. However, it will not be with the same people we used to, it will happen less frequently, and it will be more focused on specific areas. That's why there is this feeling of farewell hanging in the air...

The Swedes are going, the Americans are coming. And we go on working as we have always done – in favor of an increasingly stronger, sustainable, and diversified Volvo do Brasil. All cultures are welcome. All learning enriches. All challenges lead to growth.

The bottom line is that, regardless of nationality, we all belong to the same group and have the same corporate culture. We fight for the same ideals and strive for the same results. We are all on the same boat: the Viking one. The company continues being Swedish, with the same values and principles we have always admired and under the light of which we grew and bore good fruits.

At this moment of transition, which generates high levels of expectation and, at the same time, opens up countless possibilities, we can only say two things: to the Swedes, "Thank you very much," and to the Americans, "Welcome!"

24

The future designed

The future doesn't scare us – quite the opposite, in fact. It appears to be filled with opportunities and great challenges. But we must be prepared. After all, it is waiting for us right around the corner...

We usually make plans for five or ten years ahead as if these were going to take very long. But, at the speed in which things happen nowadays, this time goes by in a blink. The world of tomorrow comes quickly through different ways and, if we do not pay attention, we may be run over by it. That's why the sooner we begin to think about the future in a structured way, the better prepared we will be when it gets here and the more conditions of influencing it in our favor we will have.

Many people say that the future is uncertain, totally unpredictable, and that it is useless to try to project it. I believe that, in part, they are right. We cannot foresee precisely what will happen tomorrow, not even with a state-of-the-art crystal ball. But this should not prevent us from thinking about what may happen over the next years.

Drafting the future is just a matter of perception, of accurately reading and interpreting what is around us. To this end, we just have to raise our heads and look around; listen carefully to what people are saying, defending, and striving for as individuals, organizations, and society; pick up the signals that the world is issuing in different sectors. We need to observe carefully the drivers, the forces, and the trends to see where they are pointing to. Probably, that is where the future lies – maybe a little more to the right or to the left. It doesn't matter. We are not looking for scientific accuracy. We just want to identify which way the world is turning and what the prevailing issues are.

Strong trends can hardly be controlled or stopped. Most of them are irreversible, like fire uphill. The world of the future, however, will not be just a continuation of the trends of the present. New variables will appear on the horizon brought by the winds of innovation and discovery. To deal with them, new tools and skills will be needed. At the same time, looking back can also be useful. It will help to understand the evolution that has taken place in different areas and to consolidate the learning.

When I raise my head and look around, I perceive several trends in the automotive segment that will probably never stop impacting on our business, on the HR area, and on the labor relations in the future. Some of them are already affecting us today, to a greater or lesser extent, as can be seen below:

- A greener world. A demand for products with a lower environmental impact and for legislations that increasingly protect the environment. Higher awareness of people regarding this issue.
- The quest for solutions that facilitate human mobility, by deploying new technologies and processes in different means of transportation.
- The ongoing growth of the automotive segment. The truck market doubling every ten years in Brazil. More onboard technology, with all the effects that come along. More control of emissions.

- Growing demand for alternative fuels, which are cleaner and come from various sources.
- Increasing interactivity. The networks and social media are forcing companies to rethink their way of advertising, of marketing products and services, and of relating to different audiences.
- Growing presence of imported products in South America, mainly from Asia. China will probably become the world's number one economy shortly.
- Growth and development of South America, even though having business in some of these countries today is a bit like being inside a ghost train: one scare after another. Brazil, however, forges ahead at full steam. The World Cup and the Olympic Games are already waving to us on the horizon.
- Increasing pressure from society for ethical conduct and for socio-environmental responsibility actions by companies.
- The aging of the population, with major impact on the retirement system: the number of retirees grows as the number of contributors shrinks. Health insurance is becoming more expensive, due to the new technologies deployed in the treatments.
- Transition of generations in companies in a better planned and more conscious way. Preparing the successor is already seen as a natural part of this process. The well-planned retirement has become a passport to a new life, with much more quality.
- Valuing of diversity in the labor force, not only in terms of gender, age, or ethnic origin. The inclusion of people with disabilities, initially by virtue of the law, has generated new demands. Increasing participation and contribution from women.
- People and knowledge being considered the key success factor in companies. Higher requirements with respect to competencies and skills. Work relations becoming more human. More flexibility in the work environment.

- Shortage of manpower, particularly in some regions of the country. Low level of unemployment and lack of qualified professionals. In the freight carrier segment, the lack of drivers is already a reality.
- Increases in the purchasing power of the lower strata of population – the famous social bonus.
- New technologies enabling new forms of work and professional development: home office, e-learning, distance education etc.
- The quest for innovation – not as a fashion, but for pure need. Doing the same and expecting different results no longer works.
- HR with increasingly more strategic action and involved in the business.

These are some of the drivers already perceived today and that will probably be felt even more strongly in the future. They will shape the world of tomorrow. That's why they must be put on the agenda, and actions that go in this direction must be planned. Anyone wishing to harvest good fruits tomorrow must be willing to plant them today.

Man stepped on the moon and left his mark there because at some point he dreamed and believed that it was possible. As a company, we believe we can leave our mark not only on the roads of this country but also in building the world of the future. To this end, we will have to face challenges. Some have already been announced by the trends, others have never been imagined nor experienced.

In addition to preparing ourselves for what lies ahead, we have another important task to perform: think about those things that we don't want to carry into the future, analyze carefully what makes no sense to continue doing and adds no value anymore. Before moving to the new closet, we must remove from the old wardrobe the clothes that no longer fit us. Otherwise, the change will be merely on the outside. Inside, everything will continue exactly as it is – and this is no solution.

We do not want to disembark in the future carrying under our arms worn-out formulas, ideas, concepts, organizational structures, and processes, which are no longer useful. Therefore, before embarking on this voyage, we must carefully assess what to take in our baggage.

With enthusiasm, I also pack my personal baggage and catch a glimpse of the situations I will have to face to achieve the future I have designed. However, when I begin to calculate how much time I may still live, based on the life expectancy in Brazil, my enthusiasm undergoes a small seismic event.

But then the voice of hope whispers to me that perhaps I am one of those people to be benefited with an additional bonus, which will allow me to go on living for a long time. The voice of reason, however, quickly reminds me that regardless of that this time will also be limited. After all, it is the voice of wisdom that speaks the loudest: it is not the number of years but rather the quality and intensity of what I am going to live that will make the difference. And this brings peace to my heart.

At the same time, I realize that the challenges I will have to face from now on are no longer the same ones that made part of the future that I had designed in the past. Career, position, social condition, and other status symbols now give way to items that are less glamorous and have nobler purposes – only the financial reserve, outcome of careful planning undertaken throughout my life, remains on the list.

Physical and mental health, peace of mind, energy to do the things that give me pleasure and that my financial conditions allow, true friends, more family time, strengthen my spirituality, do some volunteer work, help building the world where the new generations are going to live – these are some of the challenges that smilingly wave at me in the beginning of my journey towards tomorrow. With confidence, I wave back and take the first steps.

Volvo do Brasil also moves confidently towards the future – and with a good plan under its arms, which addresses at least the next ten years. Project 2020, launched in 2010, endeavors to anticipate the look of the company in the future in terms of products and services, sales and production volumes, number of employees, infrastructure, competencies, and other organizational aspects. Characterized by dynamism, this project is being updated annually based on the changes happening in the world and on the needs and trends that arise.

It serves as a basis for the strategic plan of each business area and of the company as a whole. It is also shared with our dealer network, which uses its data as input for the Dealer of the Future project – and vice versa. This way, the plans of the dealers are permanently aligned with those of the plant.

As a result of Project 2020 and of the next ones that are already beginning to be formulated, a number of investments have been approved with a view to preparing the organization for the future, because it is not enough to get there. We must get there in good conditions, preferably in even better ones than today.

At Volvo do Brasil we live the present intensely, but we never forget to look to the future. We must be in tune with the changes happening in the world and, together with our partners, build the future we all desire and deserve.

In this sense, Brazil also deserves to be more than the land of samba, carnival, and football. The eternal country of the future has already shown it has competence to be the country of the present. That's what we believe in and what we work for.

25

And life goes on

We have thirty-five years of history and a lot to be proud of. Success did not come by chance. It was built step by step, through hard work and great determination. We faced challenges and embraced opportunities. As a result, we managed to transform our dreams into reality. We were able to feel, in several dimensions, the sweet taste of victory.

We were blessed with a rich heritage of values and principles that came to us through the kind hands of the Swedes. In the light of this legacy, we took our first steps, grew up, and built the culture of Volvo do Brasil – a mixture of the Brazilian culture and the Volvo Group's.

We created a highly inspiring work environment, which stimulates our employees to grow and develop. The belief that people make the difference permeates all our personnel policies and is translated into concrete behaviors and actions. In return, we count on a motivated and highly engaged staff.

We continually share our business plans and ambitions. Everyone has a clear view of the North to be followed. We live in a "corporate condominium", where it is possible to integrate different areas, processes, and knowledge, with the purpose of obtaining synergy, reducing costs, and maximizing results.

We count on strategic partners throughout our business chain. They are the ones who provide support for our journey, not only with their technical competencies but also with a high degree of professionalism and loyalty.

As a company of good, we have a strong sense of social responsibility, which lead us to perform countless actions in this respect. We also have a permanent commitment to a more sustainable world. We work hard to produce increasingly less pollutant and safer vehicles that meet the needs of our customers and of society.

We maintain a channel of communication always open to all audiences. We move around the business world with a lot of ethics. We do not compromise it for any reason. We want everyone who relates to us to feel this. If by any chance they don't, they should please tell us. Our actions must always speak louder than our words.

We are today a world-class company. We have become a reference in Brazil and in the Volvo world for a number of practices. We have achieved excellent results. We have earned the admiration and respect of different audiences. Therefore, we have the feeling that our homework has been done – and very carefully.

But the world does not stop. And we cannot simply lie back on our achievements and relax. We must continue working with a lot of seriousness and planning, if we want the accomplishments to keep on coming. Today's success, by itself, cannot ensure tomorrow's success.

When we look to the future, however, we feel confident. We know the map of the stepping stones. We have consistent and well-drafted plans that target at the sustainability of the company.

I participated actively in drafting these plans. I helped to design the future that we all desire. However, when this future arrives, I will no longer be part of the scenario – at least, not as an employee. My journey in the corporate world has already lasted a bunch of time, as people from my hometown used to say. I have a lot more kilometers covered than to be covered. Therefore, I will carry on with the company for a few more years and then I will start a new phase in my life: the retirement one.

When I look back, I feel very proud of the journey that I have traveled side by side with the company. We have grown together like good companions, one challenging the other. In many moments, our stories interlaced with each other. Volvo do Brasil achieved its objectives and is today a high-performance company, with a strong reputation. I have also achieved my targets and built my story. I managed to accomplish my dreams. I made it to where I wanted to be.

Some may think I did nothing exceptional. After all, I didn't put together any highly profitable business, I didn't invent anything spectacular, nor did I accumulate a great fortune. However, others who, like myself, came from the countryside to the big city in search of better opportunities, who experienced the joys and annoyances of living in a communal house, who had to count every penny to pay their bills at the end of the month, who studied often until late at night, and who managed to achieve their dreams with the outcome of their own work know exactly what I'm talking about. Today, when I see myself participating in the most important decisions of a large multinational, I realize I went much farther than I had imagined when I used to shine shoes on the village square.

And now, following the natural flow of life, I begin the process of closing my professional career. This year, according to the current rules, I officially entered the Volvo retirement preparation program, of which I was the mentor and major defender.

In my view, at the moment of my retirement I will only be getting off one train and getting on another. But the trip will continue. There are many horizons to be explored, and I will certainly have much more time, tranquility, and maturity to do this. Even though I have been using the surname of the company for so many years, I have never stopped being what I have always been: myself. This is my true identity, the one that will accompany me in this new phase of my life and that will remain with me until the end of my journey on this planet.

The company will continue its journey towards continuity on the market, sounder and stronger for the work and contribution of each one who took part in its history and left their mark on it. At the same time, it will be continually renovating, opening space for the new generations that are coming, and keeping the flame of vitality always burning.

The fact that I have started the process of preparation for retirement does not mean at all that I will decrease my level of commitment and delivery over the next few years. Quite the contrary, it is exactly in this phase that I intend to give my best, like in the last kilometers of a marathon. I want to put all my knowledge and experience at the service of the company. I wish to contribute even more for it to become a fertile soil where the new generations will be able to plant their dreams and see them germinate – like I did one day. Only then will I cross the finishing line with the feeling of duty done.

Volvo do Brasil is also coming to the end of a phase in its history that was built step by step under the attentive and competent eyes of the Swedes. It begins now, with the Americans, a new cycle in its trajectory. Our chances of success are even higher, given that we are no longer beginners. We have thirty-five years of experience under our belt and a beautiful résumé in our favor.

We count on dedicated, committed, and engaged employees, who have the firm purpose of making things happen. The transition of generations is being done in a planned manner, with no loss of the accumulated experience and knowledge. Brazil also displays a positive scenario and moves towards a future filled with possibilities. It is considered today the country where companies should be – and we have been here for quite a long time.

All paths point to success. But for it to effectively happen, we must take care of the human side of the organization, given that people are the ones who sustain and give life to our plans and dreams. This, however, is not the only reason. We will carry on treating people like people, as we have always done, because we cannot escape our essence: we are, by nature, a company with heart and soul – a Swedish soul and a Brazilian heart.

[illegible] this new phase of my life [illegible] the end of my journey on this planet.

[illegible] will continue its journey towards [illegible] for the work and commitment [illegible]

[illegible]

Volvo [illegible] that was built step by step [illegible] the Swedes; it begins now with the Americans [illegible] tory. Our chances of success are even better, given that we are not beginners. We have [illegible] years of experience [illegible] beautiful results in our history.

We count on dedicated, committed, and engaged employees, who have the firm purpose of making things happen. The transition of generations is being done in a planned manner, with no loss of the accumulated experience and knowledge. Brazil also displays a positive scenario and moves towards a future filled with possibilities. It is considered today the country where companies should be – and we have been here for quite a long time...